Emerging
HEART

Emerging Heart

Global Spirituality and the Sacred

BEVERLY LANZETTA

FORTRESS PRESS
MINNEAPOLIS

EMERGING HEART
Global Spirituality and the Sacred

Cover image: Stained glass detail, Troyes, France. Photo © The Art Archive/Eglise Sainte Madeleine Troyes/Dagli Orti
Cover design: Abby Hartman
Book design: Ivy Palmer Skrade

Library of Congress Cataloging-in-Publication Data
Lanzetta, Beverly.
  Emerging heart : global spirituality and the sacred / Beverly Lanzetta.
     p. cm.
  Includes bibliographical references and index.
  ISBN 978-0-8006-3893-1 (alk. paper)
  1. Spirituality. I. Title.
  BL624.L355 2007
  204—dc22
                                          2007002946

The paper used in this publication meets the minimum requirements of American National Standard for Information Sciences—Permanence of Paper for Printed Library Materials, ANSI Z329.48-1984.

Manufactured in the U.S.A.

Contents

For Bill

Chapter ONE

Introduction

My excursion into what I call today "global spirituality" began over thirty years ago with a series of intense and life-changing religious experiences. Growing up in a religiously liberal Catholic family, my childhood contained elements of the more expansive spiritual perspective I later embraced. However, it was not until the Divine consumed my heart and soul with a vision of immense longing that I consciously embarked on the path I write about in this book. Even then, it took many more years for me to find the words to speak about and to share my experience with others. In the context of my life, I have been blessed to meet so many sojourners along the way who have aided my journey. My first and sole companions were the mystics, whose voices reached a place in my soul untouched by daily events. John of the Cross and Ibn al' Arabi seemed to know me better than any living person I knew. So did Teresa of Avila and Mirabai. They spoke to a depth of reality that I lived in and struggled to express. The questions they posed and the insights they had into life reached into a dimension of consciousness that I can only describe with words of reverence and praise. Perhaps most comforting and healing was their unabashed love for the Divine, and their intention to devote their lives in adoration of this one, most necessary, reality.

For a number of years, my journey was a solitary one. However, in the early 1980s I felt called to pursue graduate education, completing my master's degree in sociology and human rights. Following this trajectory, in the fall of 1984 I began doctoral studies in religion and international relations at the University of Virginia. However, my first semester was turbulent as my dear dad was struggling with a terminal diagnosis of multiple myeloma. Also, I woke up each morning with whole paragraphs in my head on the mystical journey—later to become my first book, *Path of the Heart*—unrelated to the academic papers I was supposed to be writing.

My decision in 1985 to leave the field of politics to pursue my doctorate in historical theology under Professor Ewert Cousins was fateful. During my first conversation with Dr. Cousins, he gave me a paper he had written on the meeting of mystical paths and the Axial Period. I remember devouring the text at an Italian deli across the street from Fordham's Rose Hill campus in the Bronx. I was exhilarated and nourished by what I read. Crossing back to campus, I sat down on the steps in front of Keating Hall, and a voice, larger than myself, said, *"This is it!"*

Having spent so many years alone listening to the words of mystics long since passed away, I was both delighted and shocked to discover that not only were there other living people who shared my concerns, but also whole fields of academic study committed to religious dialogue and global ethics!

I rejoiced in the wisdom of contemporary thinkers—Raimon Panikkar, Abraham Joshua Heschel, Dorothy Day, Thomas Merton, M. K. Gandhi, Howard Thurman, Ewert Cousins, Huston Smith, and others—who challenged religious isolationism and championed interreligious cooperation. Similarly, I was tremendously grateful for the lineage of Christian theology and its mystical languages, as well as the heritage of the profound variety and beauty of the other religions of the world. So much of what I studied helped me to build a bridge from what I knew interiorly to the language shared by other communities of dialogue and meaning.

> *Blessed be you, impenetrable matter: you who, interposed between our minds and the world of essences, cause us to languish with the desire to pierce through the veil of phenomena.*[1]
>   Pierre Teilhard de Chardin

If we imagine ourselves standing on a mountaintop and surveying human history, we will see that every major shift in planetary consciousness began with a series of new revelations for the world. Each of these fundamental shifts in worldviews fueled subsequent generations, providing the matrix of meaning and structure of consciousness within which the next phase of civilization took root and grew. Abraham stands out as one who heralded the coming of a spiritual reality so complex and comprehensive that more than five thousand years of earth history have not exhausted it. Similarly, the enlightenment of Buddha and the incarnation of Christ have so impregnated the human imagination that it is impossible to conceive of Asian or European civilizations without their imprint. But in our own time, is there a new vision, a revelation, a truth so compelling, so vast that it will become a founding moment of a new type of human consciousness and community? Is there a breaking in of the sacred for us today? Who are its prophets? Who are its saints? How can we learn to live and practice it?

We find evidence all around us that a new planetary consciousness is taking shape now, in this moment. In conversations with students and with people I meet at conferences, on planes, and in daily human interactions, I am struck by how many people are *living* in a new spiritual landscape. With many college-age students, I sense that they were born into this new reality—their beings already *embody* it—and they literally do not live in the same psychic space as previous generations. In discussions with middle-age and older adults, a common factor is the struggle to extricate themselves from a worldview that is no longer productive or fulfilling for their spirits. Frequently, this struggle involves intense questions concerning their religious upbringing, previously held theological beliefs, or alienation from traditional spiritual forms. The process of self-discovery propels many of these people to explore traditions other than those of their religion of birth, while others reconnect with family religious values that have lapsed or been ignored.

As a human community, we are in the birth pangs of a global spiritual experiment. A recent offspring in the lineage of earth's historical traditions, this new form of consciousness both integrates and radicalizes our past, challenging us to forge new wisdom traditions. The old divisions between spirit and matter, sacred and profane, and divinity and humanity no longer can explain or assist how we need to live. Rather, they cede to an integral understanding of the cooperative building of the world that involves all dimensions of life working together in relationships of reciprocity and trust. Our minds and hearts are expanding to hold this complex vision that requires us to let go of old dichotomies and conflicts. Instead, we are challenged to think in more intricate and unified ways, integrating diverse fields of knowledge: mind-body-spirit; earth-humans-divinity; spirit-body-medicine; ecology-economics-poverty-spirit.

In this turn toward global spirituality, we traverse a new era in human consciousness, one reminiscent of what the historian Karl Jaspers termed the "Axial Period." Jaspers contended that between 800 and 200 BCE, "the fundamental categories within which we still think today, and the beginnings of the world religions, by which human beings still live, were created."[2] Heralded by the great minds of the world's civilizations—Socrates, Confucius, Zoroaster, Isaiah, Buddha, Lao Tzu—the Axial Period produced a new mode of consciousness that was instrumental in the shift from the communal worldview held by indigenous peoples to one that emphasized individual identity and self-reflective spirituality. It was also in this period that analytical and critical thought became the dominant mode of consciousness, suppressing and superseding the mythic wisdom of tribal cultures.

Ewert Cousins, for one, contends we are in the throes of a Second Axial Period, exemplified by the convergence of religious traditions and a feminine mode of consciousness.[3] Everything we know and everything we are is pushed to the limits of comprehension as a new reality—perhaps one that is immensely primeval—breaks into our world. This Second Axial Period is transforming the foundation of what it means to be human and is affecting the social, economic, religious, and cultural orientation of current civilizations and others yet to be born. To go forward, our ancestral wisdoms can aid our journey but are not alone sufficient to lead us into this unfolding era. Birth, of course, never waits for our acceptance or understanding but shocks us with embodied mystery by defying understanding. As we push and labor into new truths—perhaps a new Axial Age, or if not that, then a demand for our expanded humanity—we find ourselves traveling through territory that is, in many ways, yet to be explored.

Spanning the horizon of these last centuries, we might say that indigenous cultures lived within a revelatory world that was earth-inspired and tribal, developing a communal religious worldview that honored spirit in all dimensions of life. Here, religion emerges out of community and is embedded in the cosmos and in the cycles of nature. The Axial Period, in contrast, ushered in an age of self-reflective, spiritual inquiry that was more mind-inspired and gave rise to the individual religious quest of Buddhism, Judaism, Christianity, Hinduism, Taoism, and the other world religions. Religious consciousness became more complex and metaphysical, as well as literate and analytical, as the archetype of the individual spiritual journey became paramount in the religious imagination.

This new age unfolding in our midst points toward the emergence of a spiritual renaissance in planetary culture that is ushering in a global consciousness and a greater appreciation for the intersection of the sacred and secular. Cousins sees it as a paradigm leap or mutation in human consciousness that is heart-inspired and predicated on an integral, unifying convergence of realities. Drawing together the indigenous peoples' wisdom of the earth with the critical reflective consciousness of the Axial Period, global spirituality is self-consciously mystical and nonviolent in its orientation. As it dialogues with and incorporates the wisdom of diverse religious worldviews into its purview, this new age of spirit is directed not to religion per se but toward the contemplative structures that give rise to religious consciousness.

Much work needs to be done to understand and document the effect this common spirituality has on the inner life of the person—including faith experience, spiritual processes, prayer life, self-development—in relationship to and realization of one's ultimate source. In a forthcoming book, I will address the theologies and practices that encourage, sustain, and support the *emerging hearts* of those who are committed to global spirituality. In the pages of this book, my intention is to trace the mystical contours of this faith within/without religion, to track its movement as it emerges out of the inner core of the person, through the life of the individual, and into the world of religion, politics, and commerce. It is my dream that as we come to understand the hidden stirring of our hearts, we will find a shared spiritual grammar and a shared spiritual vision—that is not religion as we know it—that intersects with and advances the living stream of humankind's diverse religious heritage.

This book is the fruit of these many encounters and conversations. It brings together stories from students and from my personal mystical journey, with what I have learned from the great minds of ancient and contemporary religious thought on the importance of the spirit to the future of our planet.

Chapter TWO

The Days of Awe

It was October 1976, a coastal autumn filled with early morning fogs that yawned themselves away under the noonday sun. I marveled at nature's gift of flowers and yellow melons and tomatoes bursting full from vines. I had never seen a garden that rose up in full dignity from the ground, where brightly colored zinnias and columbines poked up amid summer squash and the borders were guarded by rows of marigolds. As I breathed in the salty ocean dew, the fragrant light of Sebastopol filled my vision. I did not know that God had brought me here to break open my heart and claim me for her own.

I strode across the garden path and up the stairs to the porch, listening to the wood planks creak as I made my way toward the door. Inside, the potbelly stove filled the cottage with warm hues, drawing the chill away from the uncurtained windows. I remember doing nothing in particular, when all at once I had a piercing inner sight, as if I were jerked clean out of my own reality. In an instant, I saw something, something I was not allowed to speak—or rather, that I did not know how to speak. The sight came fast, almost too fast for my thoughts to grasp, of our wounded hearts that pour love out in blotchy drabs. I saw how daily we deflect each other from loving for fear of being unloved. We seem unable to fully love; we cannot give ourselves to love. I felt the pain of our "no," a pain that pierced right into the core of my heart. I knew something about that fear; I had felt it before. It breathed upon my neck ,skirting every attempt at evasion. It came right at me; it wanted to consume me. But in an instant, I knew it totally and grasped its essence.

At that moment, it seemed the room in which I was standing ebbed away and I was washed up with the tide onto another shore. My sight, so long cast down by the curtain of convention, was unveiled. I cannot tell you what happened then, for it happened so fast, but I was literally brought to my knees and then to the ground by the intensity of what I witnessed. When the veils of reality parted, an intense suffering consumed my body. The wounded heart I saw became everyone's wound, and the sight of this suffering broke open *The Suffering*. In wave after wave, *The Suffering* flowed into me in a tidal wave of pain, passing through the pores of my soul. So intense was the pain that my heart broke open onto the plain of emptiness and I was a host upon which the suffering world fed.

In a kaleidoscope of brilliant darkness too immense to comprehend, I was shown the cause of suffering and the nature of suffering. No, *I* was the cause and the nature of suffering. Every suffering was my suffering: I was the stricken, emaciated child in Ethiopia, the mother in El Salvador whose infant has no food, the Jews marched to the gas chambers in Auschwitz and Treblinka, and the battered woman in Somalia. Every child who cries, every soldier killed in war, every tree sacrificed, every animal treated cruelly, every father who mourns, and every woman violated, was my suffering. As the hours passed, the suffering became more intense until my breath was its breath, and my heartbeat was the measure of its pulse. Tossed in the whirlwind of human violence, an unbearable pain racked my heart and my throat. I was God suffering. The Holy One suffered; God suffered the suffering. The suffering ravaged my soul. It annihilated me and left me vulnerable and spent. I died in the suffering. I died suffering. There was no me.

The pain of seeing the suffering God, the Divine who suffers, was almost more than my heart could bear. The pain of experiencing that Holy Mystery suffers and we do nothing to alleviate this suffering killed me. Having witnessed the brutality of the world and the tender mercy of God, I am nowhere free from this sight. Forever stamped and wedded to her plight, I have seen the wounded heart of the Divine.

I

> *I am waiting for you in the darkness and the great silence.*[1]
>
> ↪ Thomas Merton

As the hours passed and afternoon ceded to night, the suffering itself—its explosive power forever changing who and what I am—became the catalytic force of entrance into a new world of wisdom and delight. Impressed into my being and the cells of my body came a presence so comprehensive and a light so intense that they were concrete—more apparent than a person sitting before me, more substantial than a mountain outside my door. As real to me today as it was then, God claimed my whole existence with an intensity of divine energies so powerful and concrete that I was tangibly fused with the ground. Not an ordinary light—but a heavy, dense light more brilliant than the sun—turned its illuminative force upon me and darkened my existence in its wake, restructuring and reanimating the spirit of my body and the memories of my soul.

Annihilated by an act of transcendence, compelled by divine sight, I was held by a rapture total and complete. In this fathomless bliss of divinity, this radiant splendor too beautiful for words, all suffering was anointed and bathed in an immense joy. Stamped into whatever it is we name "*I am*" was a vast openness, a heart concealed within a heart. Coursing through the veins of consciousness was the fiery flame of another way. More than loving, it was a new way of love; more than adoring, it was a new way of adoration. The site of our sinlessness, this was the love and adoration from which all blessing flows. Indeed, the grandeur of the holy is what makes the wounds we inflict so painful, as it is divine benevolence that frees us from sin and pain.

All of reality was consumed by the strength and gentleness of a silence too rarified for language and too elusive for words. In the luminescent darkness, the silence defied and exceeded any truth yet spoken and knew with an unknowing every word uttered. As the watch of the night passed, a new revealing was taking form, as I knew without words that I had no words with which to know. Between concealment and disclosure, in the hiddenness that reveals, was a vast knowing untouched by thought. Concealed within life itself was a unifying force drawing everything into oneness. All creation was one interdependent and holy community with a unity of purpose founded in love. The sight of this profundity and the emotion of this immensity forever dispelled the fears we humans harbor of eternal sorrow or pain.

Our world is drastically amiss and critically out of line with this vision. I knew, even then, this journey into uncharted territory would not be easy or filled only with moments of bliss. I also knew that its truth was within us, buried beneath our social limitations and psychological justifications. This knowledge aroused the greatest trepidation of all, for the territory that required scouting, mapping, and ultimate discovery was the continent of our hearts.

II

Come; we'll remain a little while in silence.[2]
      Rainer Maria Rilke

A number of years later I asked Rabbi Judith, a colleague of mine at Grinnell College, if she could locate the day of my awakening on the Jewish calendar. I was not surprised when she told me that it followed on the eve of Yom Kippur after the period known as the Days of Awe. Not Jewish by birth, I have been nonetheless inextricably connected to Jewish tradition, first growing up in a predominately Jewish neighborhood and then later in being drawn to the High Holy Days. In a ten-day period—marked on one side by the Jewish New Year of Roshashana, and on the other by Yom Kippur, the most solemn Day of Atonement—God, blessed be he, say the Jews, opens the gates of heaven and becomes ever more present. This is the holy space given to repent and to receive atonement for the sins we humans commit against the hidden glory.

It has been said as well that this is the time of *Shekhinah*, the feminine indwelling presence of God, who comes out of exile to dwell among her people. The Jewish mystics claim that *Shekhinah* chose to remain with humanity after the expulsion from the garden and that She suffers voluntary exile until all creation is redeemed. Belonging to both the heavenly and the earthly worlds, She is the heart of God who feels the tragedy of the human condition, as well as Wisdom who shows us the way back to our Creator. Perhaps because She has been hidden for too long and co-opted by dominant religious cultures, I refuse to name her. I prefer my *Shekhinah* to remain nameless, a smoldering ember slowly burning up my heart.

Yet it was not the God of the Hebrew Bible I saw that day. On the other side of *Suffering* was not Moses' vision of YHWH, the Christian Jesus, the Hindu Ishvara, Buddhist *sunyata* (nothingness), nor the Muslim's Allah. I was not given to speak of God by name, calling Holy Mystery Messiah, Kuanyin, Krishna, Great Spirit, Yahweh, Tao. I do not know how to speak about an intimacy so total no words are formed in its flow. Nor how to pay homage to a generosity so vast that all gifts pale in comparison. How can I offer adoration to an ultimate reality that encompasses all beings and is the living vein of consciousness itself? The God of my heart who prefers namelessness teaches me unsaying. The God of my darkness shows the way of undoing, unbeing, and letting go. In the Divine without name and the splendor of a Reality too transcendent and too immanent to be contained, I survived the open radiance of awe. Like mirrors reflecting each other through a prism of veils, every embodiment was a transitory presence of the illusive fragrance of the Beloved. To say that I was lifted up in reverence only accumulates my shame of speaking of it at all.

III

I have been bound to this world in a single bond
with the Blessed Holy One.[3]
ᴂ—ᴓ Zohar

Now many years later, the days of awe are the fulcrum upon which my life pivots. Every experience is interpreted through the lens of what I witnessed on that fateful day. The way I think about it today is that a door, sealed from memory, burst open and I was drawn into an unnamed and untouched truth. For many years, I wrestled with how to depict what I witnessed without designating any final, identifying term. Early on, I applied the name Most Holy and Unnamable Presence, adding other concepts along the way, such as "interfaith" and "nonviolence." I called its truth "non–absolute truth" and realized its message was what religious scholars term "pluralism," the idea that divinity holds multiple and even incompatible realities. I reminded those who studied with me that this is a spiritual path skirting around the edge of language and being at that juncture where everything is let go.

I believe it was in 1985 that I first began to associate my experience with the feminine, beginning with a prose poem I composed on the *Descent of the Female Avatar*. Like some sweet music emanating from a celestial choir, whole rhythmic cadences poured into my mind and formed images so clear that the words are with me still: *She came forth upon the golden lights all radiant and clean, and upon her head shone the many-tendrilled majesty of insight where no mortal had ever stepped and nothing less than mystery could comprehend.* Yet just as quickly as the words tumbled out, they closed in upon themselves, shrouded in a cocoon of silence. I was left with a fragment of an unfinished ode.

Next I sketched an outline for a book on the Feminine Divine and wrote several chapters. But I found the exercise confusing, as words slipped away from my grasp and concepts grew borders so expansive that all meaning was lost. As I prepared myself to begin doctoral studies that fall, I stored the manuscript on a floppy disk and summarily erased it from my memory. It would be more than twenty years before I would find words to name some of these silences, when I finally wrote about via feminina, the feminine way.[4]

I knew then that the Reality that consumed my life was not the God of history or the God of our Fathers; it went beyond our religions and yet contained them all. I recognized later as a student of the world's religions that what I had experienced was indeed a breakthrough into new realities that were, at the same time, mysteriously bound to the spiritual traditions that have come before. This experience of the Divine was expansive, drawing me into the great river of silence from which the many streams of religious thought flow. Its central message, the unity of divine love; its primary command, no one and nothing excluded. To claim privileged truth or exclusive salvation was a form of spiritual violence that tore a wound through the divine heart.

Over the years I have tried to find expression for the sublimity of its truth and, in honor of its mystery, renounce the immediate and the conventional. It is difficult to express because no words and no system of thought capture its integrity. As new revelation, words are emptied in order to contain its flow. As new spiritual path, we enter an uncharted wilderness, for even our collective spiritual heritage does not provide all the signs and markers necessary for the journey. Slipping in the door of the heart quietly, without fanfare, its truth does not proclaim itself in loud voice or demand the adherence of devotees. It makes no proclamation; it is the end of proclamation and decree. In the sublimity and simplicity of its poetic presence, we are drawn to feel the vulnerability of creation and are compelled to bear the divine indwelling in the world. Enclosed in the warm embrace of this mothering wisdom, we are taught a kind of love so tender and merciful that our hearts are torn with longing.

IV

The whole universe is moistened with nectar,
and the truth is ready to harvest.[5]

    இ—ல Dogen

After thirty years I still find it difficult to write out of
a personal place, but it is the only way that I can adequately
explain how I came by way of a God without name or religion.
It was certainly true that the moment I read Meister Eckhart's
description of the God beyond God—the God that frees us
from God, or the God that is the freeing of God-talk—I felt an
immediate kinship. I cannot even say that my experience was or
was not an absence or a presence—the steep, serene face of the
Buddha or the Great Spirit of our Native American ancestors.
Perhaps it was a kind of all-encompassing or generalized revelatory vision that called to the structure of religious consciousness without itself being a religion. This was not the suffering
of Christ but *Suffering*, not the revelation *of* Jewish prophecy
but *Revealing*. My experience was the straining of my whole
being in longing for the Unrepresentable Presence that cannot be named. While undivided, it was everything; while I had
no self, it was every self; and in its calling and revealing, I felt
the pain of other people's longing and the love of God's being
for every other we reject. In this luminous reality, to enforce
any kind of superior or exclusive claim dishonors truth; in this
translucent unity, any rejection or segregation tears a hole in
the fabric of creation and is immensely painful.

    I have tried to put into words this wordless openness,
this rapt wide expanse of joy, this wrenching anguish. It has
been difficult. There are so many beautiful words and ideas;
they come from every frontier of language—Rilke, Dogen,
Rumi, Mirabai, Abulafia, Hildegard, Teresa—they form and
dance and coalesce around me, but they do not touch the core;

they do not capture the call that keeps coming back again and again, ripping open my heart. I have not been silent. But only in unknown courtrooms have I dared to speak: to others who have been laid low, to outcasts, like me, who cannot manage either through intention or defeat to lift themselves up to the world's success. I've heard their anguish in my own struggled quest, and I know the humiliation they survive just because they, too, are called by the One without name. Perhaps I have engineered my own demise by giving up and letting go of so many world opportunities. But I hear this call, and it yearns within me to desire it alone: Do not succumb to the marketplace of ideas or packaged religions, or even the latest and greatest theological trend.

Even though at times I longed to travel the well-trodden path, I'm not going that way. I need to use some of our shared vocabularies to make my case, to speak about the One without name who beckons and anoints us with the gift of an impossible hope—a dangerous idea today. I also have learned that in taking the risk to express these sentiments, I find many people who feel the same. Even my doctoral studies in Christian theology and mysticism were a way of exploring whether my religion without religion and my nameless spiritual life were *fully* contained within the Catholicism given to me at birth, or in any of the other wisdom traditions I studied and taught. They were not. That fact became the catalyst for a greater appreciation of the complex unity that is both the womb and the offspring of religious diversity. If I could venture a description, I would say that the breaking in of the Divine had opened up within me the structure of the religious, a reality so comprehensive and total that evidence of it was everywhere while it in itself was nowhere. This curious fact allowed me to embrace my parents' and thus my own Catholic heritage—albeit loosely practiced and upheld—and to find in it and in every other spiritual path an irreducible beauty and wisdom. I was a visitor who found respite in the folds of great mother wisdoms and in the arms of valiant father theologies. I could dwell in any religion, but I was not of it. And what I was shown or understood or perhaps remembered was this: We are so loved and embraced by the One without name that the spark of divinity in our very finite and small self is an infinite grandeur greater than any religion. No religion can contain us; every religion is subsumed under the mystical point of unity in our own deepest center.

V

> *Forsake and give up everything. Then your*
> *hearts will become wide and deep.*[6]
>   Hadewijch

    Somewhere along the way—even though for years I taught the principles or structure of this contemplative life— I ventured to find a name. Although no name was given, the way the word "interfaith" or "interreligious" is used seemed a close approximation. The idea that in interreligious dialogue we discover a reality not pre-contained in any prior truth, a reality that is accessible only through the expansion of our souls, spoke directly to my experience. I attended and was ordained by an interfaith seminary, because the principles upon which interfaith ministry are based provide an experimental atmosphere within which the mystical point of unity among all peoples and religions can be celebrated and practiced.[7]

    In 1993, the same year I was ordained, I founded the Desert Interfaith Church, followed by the Interfaith Theological Seminary in 1997. These initiatives were my way of affirming the unitary nonviolence of the spirit of creation and a way of giving others who felt the same a communal expression within which to sanctify their longing for God. The ordination was not to a religious institution or even to a community of believers. It was rather to a contemplative practice and a social and spiritual acknowledgment that the Divine now was at the center of one's life. It was a way in which the spirit anointed each person with the sanctifying grace of being called and answering "yes" to that call. For those who all their lives had been outsiders, women foremost among them, the right to be ordained by what most truly moves them, heart and spirit, is both gift and grace.

The people who joined our seminary came from every walk of life, different denominations and traditions and many professions, including nurses, physicians, college and public school educators, massage therapists, scientists, and psychologists, to name a few. Whether these spiritual people remain committed to one religious tradition or choose to be fully interfaith in orientation, a common factor is that they join countless other people around the globe who function as a collective vanguard moving into a new revelatory landscape. When I write these words, "new revelatory landscape," I mean we have been called to and are being called by a new or different paradigm of the sacred that is making fundamental demands on our personhood and view of self, God, and the world. These individuals are following a spiritual journey in the desert—to a desert spirituality—outside the bounds of time and place to come face-to-face with what moves them most deeply and opens their bodies and souls to glimpse a new unveiling of the sacred. They are living this mystical transfiguration now in their bodies, growing into the depth and breadth of what rejoices in them and tears at their hearts. They are forging through a contemplative process of enlightenment as old as life itself; and even though, and perhaps because of, the absence of a language to speak this new way, they are being transformed, like a silkworm in its cocoon turning—it knows not how—into a butterfly.

To have any identifiable name, even one as collaborative as "interfaith," can be problematic. As soon as an idea or vision takes form, there are people who want to domesticate and possess it or make it something sustaining, permanent, enduring, respectable, transmittable, something capable of being organized and, therefore, controlled. But how do you contain a *vantage point*—seeing everything from the perspective of vast intimacy such that all things are included within it, all determinate religions are the children of this immense dynamism—the pole of the religious and the a-religious?

It is not that this reality is not religious or against religion; it is just that the "religious" is already contained within it; there is no need to demarcate its presence. The sacred does not need grand adornments to dress it up or formal gowns to make it palatable. It is already and always more than we can possibly bear and far more than we can imagine. Further, there are some of us who are hermits and wanderers, who feel most comfortable in silence, on the edge, without a religious home. We cannot have a God with a name. For every name would be somehow blasphemy; and even though we honor names— Jesus, Buddha, Mohammad, Moses, Krishna, Woyengi, Corn Woman, Goddess Durga, Great Spirit—we are called to claim none as our own. This is our faith. This is our calling from that mysterious oneness *concealed within life itself.* This is our secret. But it is an open secret that cannot be contained.

At first this faith within/without religion can sound rather ominous or off-putting, like someone is rejecting another person's greatest devotion or greatest love. It would be like saying, "I love you," in the abstract but not in the particular. But, really, it is not like that. Every loving exceeds name. There is no name adequate to our love or to our beloved. That is the nature of love: to be both concrete and ungraspable; singular and universal. To love passionately the Divine without name is not to reject god, love, or names, but to measure up to the immensity of what love is: its embracing of everything and its rejection of nothing. It is to become an open vessel of intimacy, in which we offer ourselves to each other without restraint. Love gives up attachment to a particular name in order to embrace the fullness of all naming. This is not something we do or a choice we make. It is a blind stirring that leads us through the anguish of letting go and into the arms of an excessive grace; and it cannot be ignored. Life practices it everyday.

This path—that Meister Eckhart called a *"wayless way"*—is not primarily cognitive but travels through the prayers and tears of faith. It does not hail the emergence of a formal religion with its redacted canon of sacred texts. The wayless way is not the speaking of the angel Gabriel or the anointing of the Holy Virgin or the passage of night in which the Buddha finally found himself cosmically awake. It is not yet tangible; it is the moment before Jesus took up the cross, Mohammad heard a word, or Mary knew she was bearing child. It is the moment of the quickening of the Divine within; it is the revelatory, enlightenment moment that so many people feel but do not know how to speak. The path of no path is not a formula found in imitation of the past but the explosive force of new revealing now. It calls us to leave behind what we know to wander into the unknown, to the place where we are on the threshold of an inconceivable hope.

Faith within/without religion is only worth its salt when it probes questions not from the known, but the unknown; not from the remedy, but the question; not from power, but from mercy. If we do not admit we are lost, pained, hanging on the cross of our own convictions, deaf to the cries of others, and blind to the suffering at our door, how can we ever hope to sustain the breaking in of the impossible?

VI

> *How could they not bow down in adoration*
> *before thee, Thou who art all that is?*[8]
>
>   ✑✎ Bhagavad Gita

Often when people hear something of my story or learn that I am an interfaith minister, they immediately assume: she is *not* Catholic or *not* Christian. Even some of my closest friends and long-term companions on the journey still think that it is possible to repudiate one's own history, or that exclusiveness can work in reverse to assert the denial of a claim. I do not see it that way. If this new breaking in of divinity tells us anything, it is that the old tribal alliances and the unholy claims to the exclusive possession of the "one and only" truth no longer hold. Yet this illumination of countless instances of human treachery and deceit does not demand the rejection of any authentic faith, but the inclusion of all faiths in the circle of a greater love. At times I even like to say—and the saying and the times vary—that I am called to practice the silence of the Buddha, Krishna's devotion, Rumi's fasting of the heart, the nonviolence of Jesus, the wayless way of Tao, Hopi earth awareness, and Jewish *teshuvah* (repentance). This stance is not mere curiosity or wordplay. It is, instead, the realization of an experiential reality. We contain within us the whole of human spirituality, and our very selves are constituted in some way by this collective heritage. It also does not refute the divergent beliefs of the world's religions and of my own Christian roots that, for example, Jesus is an incarnated savior and one finds salvation through his way. A Muslim cleric, in an interreligious dialogue conference I organized, took exception to this stance when he asked in genuine concern how I could reconcile the Christian claim that Jesus is the incarnation of God with the Muslim view that the idea of any incarnation of divinity violates Allah's absolute transcendence, or even for that matter with the nontheistic perspective of Japanese Zen Buddhists, who name their highest reality, *sunyata*—Absolute Nothing. But from this mysterious *vantage point* I find no contradiction of intent, as the Divine—whatever it is revealed to be and whatever name we assign—does not abide by our restrictions, and who is to say that it does not, in all its generosity and abundance, give forth to multiple expressions of itself?

It is tempting, too, to label this nameless divinity and this religion without religion as a reductionism and a unitarianism that is nonsacramental and is connected to no distinct moment of awe or transcendence. Rather, that it is a kind of intellectual spiritualism without benefit of those enduring cycles of meaning and bereft of the deep and mysterious grounding that forms the charism and the spirituality found in other religions. This view, too, seems shortsighted insofar as the absence of a name and the newness of expression does not in any way rule out the influx of the sacred and the immediacy of knowing one is in the presence of holiness and grandeur. The sacramental is not excised or diminished by the breadth of the circle of adherents, but presents itself whenever one's whole being is opened to the luminous presence in the world around us or in one's core.

Sacrament informs this faith within/without religion, and it pivots around the twin moments that stamp our beings forever: the divinity of *Suffering* and the excessive gift of *Revealing*. The holiness of suffering means that divinity is so intimately intertwined with all of creation that every suffering is also divine suffering. All of the sins we commit, errors we perpetuate, and wounds we exact have a corresponding impact that is borne by the Divine. We are never alone. If we truly grasped the enormity of this vision we would bow down in sorrow and rectify the world's pains, ills, and woes. Our hearts simply could not tolerate either the violence we inflict on each other and on creation or the justifications we use to authorize and rationalize callousness or atrocity. We are bound by this suffering, and it is through and in suffering that we discover not only the principle of transcendence but also the vehicle by which we are transformed. Somehow in suffering we touch our capacity for intimacy, and the exhilaration of dying in order to be reborn, twice-born anew. For it is only through those events that shatter our view of reality that we find the courage to let go of ourselves and let God be God.

Life is a sacrament that is kissed by the spark of divinity from birth to death; there is no escaping it; there is no denying it. We can mark out central aspects of sacramentality and, like the Lakotas and Hopis, offer our newborns to the rising sun, or anoint the foreheads of infants in the baptismal waters of Christ's vocation, or take the vow of a Hindu *sannyasin* who rejects social roles and conventions for the wild horizon of renunciation. We can sanctify our marriages and authorize our priests, and pray over the dying with the fervor of conviction. We can ingest the body of Christ and find there a mysterious feeding of our souls and a radical forgiveness of our sins. All this and more we do. Sacrament is part of existence; only we humans can dim its light or deny its power. Holiness is made new now, every day, and it dwells in each one of us who—branded by the torrent of light—lay our hearts down in stilled expectation and hope.

The spirit dwells among us and we cannot stop its flow. The saffron-robed Buddhists who climbed over the crooked roads and steep hills of Cambodia to anoint the trees and to ordain them monks knew this. So did Ansel Adams, as he scaled the steep cliffs of Yosemite in tennis shoes to capture a vision of Cathedral Rock. Or Georgia O'Keefe, who transfixed the hills of Abiquiu on canvases crossed by spirit-translucent light. And the pounding waves on the shore of Mount Tamalpais, which bring us to our knees and salt away our tears. Sacrament is not confined to synagogue or mosque, but flows out into the world for those with eyes to see and hearts to feel.

There is also the excessive gift that makes us tremble and brings all of us up short—the pouring out of unbounded generosity that transforms our tired and weary hearts into something more innocent and new. Our selves are made of this excessiveness, even though we glimpse but shadows of its potential each day; and it is through this gift that cannot be possessed that we find the courage to become incandescent and noble, to live more for each other than for the self. Its meaning is traced through the touches of love we share and the intensity of human passion to know and to be known. In every quotidian ounce of life, in every smallest particle of matter, this utterly alluring gift fuels our souls. All our prayers and deepest longings trace an adoration of life for itself. We cannot but strive to speak the unspeakable. Even if we were to throw our lives upon the fire of this passion, we could never say or capture the immediacy of the gift or the extent of our devotion to the living desire that inspires our souls. Everything that is is sacramental. All of this and more that we may never feel and can never say comes from the excessive gift of love. Daily life is only a continual domestication of this longing, perhaps a continual suppression of what animates us most, a continual curtailment or clipping of the aching generosity that breaks all bonds of convention. But even so, and even when we labor to suppress the ardent exhilaration for home, we know it is futile. We are the bearers and the witnesses of the unveiled gift of glory.

Forgive me if I am less than quiet in Your namelessness.

Chapter THREE

Open Secrets

Bankei Yotaku (1622-1693), a Japanese Rinzai priest, recounts the story of his passion for truth. One day at his village school, the class was reciting Confucian texts, when the teacher came to the central words, "'The way of great learning lies in clarifying bright virtue.' Bankei interrupted the teacher. 'What is bright virtue?' he asked. The teacher, repeating the glosses given in one of the traditional commentaries, answered, 'The intrinsic nature of good in each person.' Bankei asked what the intrinsic nature of man was and was told, 'It's his fundamental nature.' 'Then what is that?' he persisted. 'The ultimate truth of Heaven,' replied the teacher.' None of these answers satisfied Bankei. A deeper explanation was needed. He wanted to know what bright virtue really meant in terms of his own practical experience."[1]

Bankei became consumed by religious doubts. Soon he began to lose interest in his studies and stopped attending school. In exasperation, his brother banned him from the house. Thus, at the young age of eleven, Bankei was homeless. Over the ensuing years, he took his inquiry to Confucian scholars and Buddhist priests and traveled to various Zen monasteries for instruction. He subjected himself to all kinds of spiritual austerities and physical deprivations. After years of hardships, his physical health was affected and Bankei was near death. Yet he could not attain the wisdom he sought. "My regret," he later wrote, "[was] dying with the great matter I've been struggling with . . . since I was a small boy, still unresolved." Resigned to death, and in the most despair of his life, Bankei suddenly—in that instant—received enlightenment: *All things are perfectly resolved in the unborn.*[2]

Zen master Bankei's relentless quest to personally experience truth is repeated in countless instances of world religious literature. From ageless time, humans have sought through direct understanding to know whether there is god or truth or any meaning in life. Seekers are never content to accept the status quo or to believe what their religions tell them without questioning, without finding their own path to the ultimate. This search and its effects are mysticism. And it is the mystical quest that underlies and informs global spirituality today.

I

> *If I have achieved anything in my life, it is because I have not been embarrassed to talk about God.*[3]
> ᘒᗏ Dorothy Day

At the time I had my encounter with the holy, I could not claim any formal knowledge of mystics or the word "mysticism." In fact, it was not until my first semester at Fordham that I began to study the field of mysticism in earnest. Over the years, I had read biographies of saints and been captivated by certain mystical writings. But I had not situated the lives of these spiritual masters within a larger historical context or associated the word "mysticism" with my October visitation some ten years before. I can remember the exact time and place that I first used the word "mysticism" in public. One of my colleagues in the doctoral program was a Benedictine sister with whom I had become friends. We were walking from our graduate seminar on fourteenth-century spirituality to our cars. I was engrossed with watching the light filtering through the lime green buds of an especially large maple tree when Sr. Joyce casually asked me, "What made you write *Path of the Heart?*" This was the manuscript that intruded into my studies at the University of Virginia and had recently been published. No one had asked me this question before. Outside of a close circle of friends, neither my family nor my colleagues knew about my spiritual conversion. Without thinking about my words, I replied, "A number of years ago I had a series of life-changing religious experiences. This book is my desire to share the mystical journey with others."

Looking back, this rather innocuous exchange marked a turning point in my willingness to speak about religious experiences. The intention to do so seemed to break an old taboo against speaking in public about one's inner life and dispelled the fear that rightly cautions against pride. In subsequent encounters with students and colleagues, I came to further respect the importance of spiritual dialogue in academic and other professional settings. As I turned my attention to Christian theology and then to contemporary religious thought, I found an intrinsic mystical perspective beneath much of the writing. The early church writers were mystical theologians, and a fair number of contemporary theologies draw explicitly from mystical teachings within their respective religions. The more I studied, the more convinced I became that the meeting of religions and the pioneering fields of interreligious dialogue and world ethics were a natural outgrowth of mystical consciousness projected onto a global context.

"Mysticism" is a notoriously difficult word to define. Like other concepts within humanity's spiritual heritage, mysticism is depicted in diverse and sometimes contradictory ways. We might find common agreement, however, in Bernard McGinn's idea of mysticism as "the immediate consciousness of the presence of God" or ultimate reality, however named or defined. This experience takes place on a level of personality deeper than the consciousness of emotions, cognition, or psyche. As McGinn noted, mystics, regardless of their religious lineage, "continue to affirm their mode of access to God is radically different from that found in ordinary consciousness, even from the awareness of God [or ultimate reality] gained through the usual religious activities of prayer, sacraments, and other rituals."[4]

Mystical texts refer to the immediacy of divine presence, witnessing to those moments when we are not in control of reality and the unimaginable breaks into our awareness, flooding our whole being with insight. It is our capacity for realization and not just knowledge, when we come face-to-face with reality and not just representations. Like a painting or a poem, mysticism reveals what *is* in a new way. By igniting the generosity and intimacy dormant in us, mysticism enflames the heart with compassion for the world. Caught up in a devotion to the divine other, mysticism traces a potential intrinsic to the better part of human nature—what we call the saintly or holy, the enlightened or realized.

Mysticism refers to what is normally understood as a "desert place." When the bottom of the soul has dropped away and the self is free to be no-self, we enter a realm of consciousness and sphere of activity that moves out of a subjectless state. Mystical consciousness, then, is the place in each of us that is constituted by and returns to the place of *nothingness* or *openness*. It is the silence within us that is older and prior to religion and deeper than the unconscious, moving in the current of benevolence and mercy. This mystical dimension is, thus, not a rarified spiritual state but a further depth dimension within all human awareness, operating alongside other ways of knowing, including the rational, intellectual, and aesthetic. The mystic in us is the knower of the unknown, see-er of the unseen, who is able to withstand—without sacrificing or abandoning love—the contradictions and confusions of the world.

We cannot escape the mystical, nor can we escape being the mystic. It is the force of creativity and innovation within us, the dream of the impossible becoming tangible, and the prophecy that needs to be told, waiting to finally burst forth and proclaim itself. Mysticism is not a demanding or dogmatic state, but travels in low places suffering and rejoicing in the trenches of all that life offers and takes away. This heightened sensitivity to spirit is a teaming possibility rooted in the structure of consciousness itself. It is the rushing up of the desert place that moves us from some hidden cavern in our own beings. Here, the spirit in us cocreates the emergence of the new and the formation of the not-yet formed. We discover the gestational ground of our beings, bringing forth the light before dawn. To be whole, to be awake, the mystic in us is forged in the fire of our anguishes and joys until what is instinctual and spontaneous becomes focused and gathered in its own rhythm.

II

> *Rightly understood, the mystic is not a special*
> *kind of human being; rather, every human being*
> *is a special kind of mystic.*[5]
>   ᶜ—ᵉ David Steindl-Rast

Usually when I teach a course on comparative mysticisms students ask a lot of questions. They want to know what mysticism is, and many of them are skeptical of what appears to be rather unscientific or irrational. In class discussions, I listen to impassioned debates between students who are empowered or challenged by this new horizon of experience. Without exception, however, in every course a student tracks me down to pose a similar question: *Am I a mystic?* One such person was Kevin, who stands out in my memory as unusually quiet and forthright. An engineering student who was taking Mysticism and Human Experience as part of his humanities requirement, Kevin approached me toward the end of the semester to discuss an experience he had the previous summer off the California coast. He recounted that one evening he climbed on his surfboard under the light of the moon. The sky was clear and millions of stars were visible. He paddled out farther than he had gone before and at some point found himself floating on a calm sea. As far as his consciousness extended, he was rocked by the gentle undulation of the waves and the sounds of the distant surf. Troubled by the failure of his first relationship and by parents who criticized his educational aspirations, Kevin was inconsolable that night. Suddenly, in the still darkness, he was stunned by an intense light illuminating his mind. For a moment, he was scared. But, then, the light filled him with the "greatest sense of belonging" he had ever felt. Although alone, drifting in the vast ocean on nothing more than a fiberglass board, he felt united with everyone and everything. He was somehow, and in some mysterious way, immeasurably blessed. The intensity of what he felt and knew was transformative, placing his life and present troubles in a wholly different context.

Although unable to make sense of his experience at the time, Kevin confided that he felt that perhaps he was a type of mystic. Like other members of the class, he harbored a common misunderstanding about mysticism—that it involves some kind of secret knowledge inaccessible to ordinary humans. Closely tied to this notion of a secret is what William James called the ineffability of mysticism—the inability to put into words what is experienced. The paradox of mysticism is that at the same time it is labeled "secret" or "ineffable," the enormity of humanity's spiritual archives attest to the fact that mysticism is not beyond human understanding but is the capacity within each of us to touch and be touched by wonder and awe.

Kevin discovered that his mystical encounter did not make him a superior being more certain of life than others. Nor did it necessarily help resolve his inner turmoil. Instead, the effect of being touched by divinity left him vulnerable and sensitive to the oneness of life and increasingly willing to let himself be aware of other universes of perception. Describing his experience as one in which he was "pierced by intimacy," Kevin felt that his ideas about who he was and what he should do were toppled by the magnitude of belonging he felt. There was nothing forced or dogmatic about his new awe of life. He had no desire to tell others what to believe or demand that God tell him what to do. Like other mystic personalities, he found himself more able to live each day in the beauty of the moment and more aware of the gratuitous gift that loves without condition and makes empty all our hollow attempts "to love."

Kevin's story is not uncommon. So many people have similar experiences. Mysticism is not reserved for special individuals. Rather, what is considered "the mystical" is accessible in the deep consciousness of every one of us. It is permission to see what is normally unseen or ignored, feel what is trivialized or suppressed, speak what is often unspeakable or denied, and know what is kept hidden or veiled. Mysticism, then, is not confined to the realm of ecstatic experiences beyond the grasp of daily existence. It is based upon a kind of awareness or sight whereby the person pays attention to glimpses and visions all around us of something other—wholly other—exceeding and exposing the limits of the everyday. The mystic in us sees and realizes the interdependence of creation that others do not see or deny having seen. Even when we do not admit or are unaware of this unity, our hearts suffer its denial and strive in action, both inner and outer, to facilitate mending the illusory divide.

When the mystic heart looks at creation, it sees the world is formed by and composed of a divine imprint everywhere present and nowhere absent. Nothing that *is* is not spirit. This is what the mystic in us *sees*; this is what the mystic in us *knows*; it is this that compels the mystic in us to celebration and lament. Sadly, we have been educated and trained to close our hearts and avert our eyes from the blazing light all around us. We pass our blindness and muteness down from generation to generation, as if we tell our newborns: *Don't see. See at your own peril.* We learn early on to hide our wisdom, to be ashamed of our vision, to suffer ridicule for our sensitivity or insight: *Don't know. Don't tell too much.* It is not the mystical that is a secret, hidden realm. It is this hiding and blinding and denying that is killing us. This is the secret that we do not want to see or hear: we are socially constituted to be "unsee-ers."

Western culture is implicated in trying to blind the eyes of the spirit. It has, in fact, destroyed or attempted to destroy those cultures that believe in "seeing," like the Hopis and the Celts, or the Maori shaman. Control over what is seen and who gets to see—and thus who is entitled to tell—is exerted by dominant cultures and groups of people over the conquered or marginalized. The mystical breaks all that open by dispelling the idea that there is a privileged point of seeing. It democratizes sight because our eye is the same as the presubjective eye that sees without having to proclaim, "I am." We see with the inner eye, before the formation of the "I," in a subjectless place—a place that the historical mystics like Meister Eckhart equate with a transcendental eye: *"My eye and God's eye are one seeing and one knowing and one doing."* The blind eye sees with the heart, feeling the vibration of meaning that binds life into wholeness and suffers over its fractures and pains.

The mystical is a breaking in moment of the unimaginable. It is also the breaking out of the mystery contained within us, an unveiling and letting go of what we already know and are. It is a moment of pure gift, when we are flooded with *The Unconditional*—with a love and wisdom that can never be repaid. The mystical comes unexpectedly—who could plan or design it?—outside and beyond what we accept or reject. It cannot be held or possessed. Rarely can it even be invoked. Awe comes, we know not how, in the woods beside still oaks, by the bed of a dying parent or friend, in the winter of our anguish when we have lost all hope, on the slope where the setting sun dips beneath the rising crest of an ocean wave. It claims us for its own, touching the depth of our beings, animating the cells of our bodies, and enflaming our longing for the inviolable. Like Bankei, we are impassioned by the storm of passion inside us and for the wonder of existence itself. We cannot even hold the immensity in our bodies for more than moments, and if we could we would not be born. The mystical flows through our veins and spills into our hearts in a torrent of desire, longing through us for the coming realization or enlightenment. It upends everything, throwing our rationed offerings and our critical analyses against the heart overwhelmed by splendor. We want to know what love would do—*what would love do?* That is the mystical.

III

> *If you open your mind's eye you will see that*
> *the Holy Spirit weeps tears of fire in every one*
> *of my servants who offers me the fragrance of*
> *holy desire.*[6]
>   Catherine of Siena

Much of our lives from birth to death are a suppression of great depth of feeling. We are socialized to control emotions, curtail excessive outbreaks of joy or sorrow, and silently suffer the effects of devastating traumas. We are taught to love, but not too much or for too long—certainly not excessively for the outsider or orphan. We are encouraged to harness our emotional depth for the world's purposes, often those that promote or advance material progress, prestige, or comfort. Spiritually, we are instructed that the sign of maturity is to have achieved a certain measure of equanimity in the face of life's events. Public displays of intense feeling are discouraged, ridiculed or ignored. True enlightenment, we are told, is supposed to transcend these transient cravings of the human personality.

Mystical awareness is more honest. It demands and requires an emotional honesty rising up from deep currents of feeling—those states deeper than psyche or unconscious when we personally experience wonder and amazement. Something in the touch of the Divine unleashes an emotional torrent that saturates our souls with a new grammar of the holy. We may suppress, deny, or try to kill this depth of feeling, but the compassion intrinsic to our own beings never goes away. We are never free of or far away from a divine level of concern. As the Divine breaks into our hearts, we feel nothing other than the unity that binds all beings together, a flooding of our cells and our senses with the magnitude of being graced. It is like opening every pore in your body, every nerve in your heart, and every fiber of your being to hold and to be embraced by an emotional intensity that can shatter your bones. It is an influx of desire for us and in us that fuels our longing for more; and it comes, when it comes, so often through suffering. The unconditional advances into our hearts when we are laid bare, when we don't know where else to turn, when we have traded in our membership in the social club for the pain of not belonging, and find the courage to just say, "Yes." Let me be. Let it all in. Show me what is.

Saint Catherine of Siena writes about the weeping of fire and the tears of fire the Holy Spirit unleashes in our minds. The weeping of fire—what a way to say it, and something only someone who has been there could write—has no tears because it is the blaze of the spirit in us, drawing us to feel our helpless, hopeless attempts to make things "right." We can all go crazy before we admit that we weep—yes we do—because of what we see and feel that breaks our hearts. This is the wound of love that flows through us and suffers in us the penetrating sweetness and unspeakable suffering of the world.

Like Catherine, St. Francis was converted by an intensity of feeling, mystical in origin. In his witness to the violence inflicted on the poor toiling in his father's textiles factories, he became "crazy" and "suspect," stripping himself naked in solidarity with lepers and serfs. Or Milarepa who, upon discovering his mother's decayed bones, fell into an infirmity of heart. Or Gandhi who felt the people of India in his own soul and thus suffered the suffering of others until he, too, was one of them—one with the poor and oppressed, one with the plight of women and *dalits* (untouchables), and even one with the poisonous snake who threatens human life itself.

We cannot help but live in a paradox where suffering lays down next to joy. We do feel and bear suffering, and not only human or sentient suffering, but also divine or mystical suffering. We experience the intentional tearing and destruction of the sacred. We understand in some hidden depth of our hearts that we humans, in a fury of despair, extinguish the hope of the holy coming into our midst. Even as we long for the return of our prophets, bodhisattvas, and messiahs, we refute or deny its possibility in our cells. What are we to do with our hopelessness? Is it a collective grieving and forgetfulness that grips us? Everything we do or do not do reverberates in the whole of creation. Even though we harbor denials and aversions, divinity permeates everything and is absent from nothing. Our hearts are tuned to the indelible sensitivity intrinsic to each creation, the luminescent light that encloses and encircles life, the scars and wounds we inflict on each other, and the stilling and killing of the sacred that never goes away. We witness the destruction of the holy and it pains our own beings with a grief that we misapprehend and refuse to name. Even though we have been conditioned to be tone deaf to the cries around us and in us that call out for justice and mercy, the Divine never goes away.

The mystical brings into speech this intensity of feeling that is unspoken and denied. It is a tremendous need in today's world where everything is reduced to either the factual or the hysterical. The unspoken and unseen to which mysticism refers is not the slippery world of untested assumptions, psychic hunches, or spiritual favors. Instead, mysticism speaks to the anguish and brokenheartedness that comes from living in a glorious and troubled world. Mystical language provides us with a way of talking about and encouraging awareness of the gratuitous miracle called *Life*. We do not have to strive for the mystical or suffer the absence of those quintessentially mystical experiences—whether of visions, locutions, or raptures—depicted in hagiographies. Its structure is already within us: as the locus of loving knowledge and the doorway into our secret feelings about life, as the compunction that grips us and the obligations that happen, and as the desire that pushes us forward toward mystery and awe.

The force of the mystical in us is catapulted through compassion and, having witnessed the Divine spark present in each thing, compels the heart toward mercy and the alleviation of injustice. The whole of the mystic temperament is caught in the pathos of the world and is never free of it, even—and perhaps more so—when the Divine wounds our hearts with love. We are swept away, but only to return to this world more aware than ever of the cries of pain and the need to comfort those who suffer. The prophets are the ones who feel this enormous responsibility—this obligation to uphold the vision fiercely felt and understood. The moments of heightened awareness or the touches of divine love come freely, attuning our hearts in the process to the precious gift of life and to the striking pain of so much of humanity. We are never outside the circle of the Divine, but always swimming in the ocean of intimacy within the joys and sorrows of existence.

Mysticism does not tell us when or how we will encounter the holy. This unknowing is the gripping, wrenching sorrow that marks the spiritual nights when the whole structure of the clinging self is brought down and there is no stable point of reference. The anguish of these great doubts and spiritual deaths is that there is no god ahead of the self that can dictate what and who will be known, seen, or experienced. In the moment of spiritual aridity—of a spiritual desert in which our hearts are brought against not knowing, not loving, not having—faith breaks the bonds of having to know and can just be faith, going it knows not where, being guided from an obscure luminescence, until everything just shimmers and leaves us gasping for air. In our blindness, groping in the dark, the feeling senses are heightened until one's whole being is nothing more than a mass of bliss and anguish, an ecstatic tearing and gnashing that no one else can see or hear. The dying that comes goes on "forever" until the I that ceases to die finally lets go, opens up, and is freed into the dying that is not death. After the fiery jubilation of love, we are branded by intimacy and able to withstand the intensity of being alive. There is no returning to close doors or to close down the habit of feeling, for now one is inscribed by and inscribed in mystery.

Our souls move from a subjectless process, prior to the unconscious, deeper than vision and thought, before our memories. Our religions name it the spark of the Divine, the hidden castle, the interior flame, nothingness, or *bodhichitta*. This is the place within us that is no longer in debt, no longer conscripted to payment and return. Even though we are given to sacrifice ego and identity, we are never outside the circle of reciprocity and the excesses of divine love. These divine gifts do not bind us to surrender for and to a God outside us, but are the flowing in of receptivity to a superior grace that can never be repaid. We are not punished or inadequate or tempted or in sin; we are simply given with an abundance that overwhelms

and humbles every "self." The inflow of benevolence can-
cels our debts, wiping away our tears and all the old retribu-
tions, karmas, and sins. We can afford moments of happiness
because the price—of the self—has already been paid. There
is no choice now. And once the giving has been truly offered,
there are only prayers and tears of gratitude and joy. Whichever road we take is *the way*; whatever comes comes from the
night of abundance, ushering in a horizon that is exorbitant,
outside of time—eccentric.

IV

> *Marvelous it is to see clearly in this moment the*
> *depth of meaning for which others journey far.*
> *There is no path or stage to traverse; there is no*
> *goal to achieve.*[7]
>
> ✐ Tilopa

Mystical consciousness offers an important corrective and
guidance for our new revelatory time. Our historical traditions
began within the context of localized geographical, social, and
spiritual environments. They took form out of specific tribal,
ethnic, and social worldviews that were necessarily singular
and communal. While offering today a universal message,
they were not in their inception principally guided by a global
vision or specifically directed to a worldwide community. Often
formed in contrast to or reaction against a dominant religious
and cultural consciousness, the world's religions have struggled
to maintain a distinctive identity and to preserve ancient lineages from destruction or attack. The contribution that mysticism has made within these historical traditions has suffered
suppression and rejection through the centuries, in large part

because the noninstitutional liberation mysticism offers is frequently perceived to be a threat to the continued survival of corporate religious identity.

For centuries, especially in Western theologies, a tension has existed between religious orthodoxy and mystical spirituality. In addition, a strong cultural prohibition is exerted against "the mystical" and against whatever probes beneath the façade of things to peer into what is more authentic and real. Social contracts are set up to contain and curtail this deeper level of feeling and seeing, to make us functionally speechless and sightless by blocking off what we are conditioned not to say or see. Culturally we do not really know what the mystical is but are intent on its suppression, warning that it may be dangerous or occult, or dismissing it as suitable only for the spiritually elevated and mature. These objections are convenient insofar as they uphold a certain social order that permits and maintains the illusion of personal awareness even as we educate and train for collective amnesia.

However, what may have served as a preserving or guarding function over these centuries now is in danger of standing in the way of the urgent necessity in our time for a shared spiritual vision sustainable not just for our souls, but for the flourishing of life itself. Consistently relegated to the margins of cultural discourse over much of Western history, mysticism most recently has been ridiculed by proponents of various contemporary "isms"—postmodernism, fundamentalism, materialism, capitalism—as a naïve return to the past, a corrosive element in the churches, or a kind of sloppy New Ageism. Like much that passes for wisdom today, this depiction of mysticism is both hasty and wrong. If mysticism stands for anything, it is this: an extended vision of the integral animating force, or interdependent unity, which is the real existence of everyone and everything.

This sad situation has spawned generations of people who are uninformed about spiritual resources within their own traditions and uneducated in the rudimentary spiritual dimensions of their lives. Religions, by retaining a dichotomous understanding of transcendence and immanence, and sacred and profane, control access to the sphere of the sacred. This authoritarian strain, which seems to infect every religious tradition, maintains vigilance over personal attempts to access the Divine directly, often dismissing as misguided or even heretical those individuals who press against the boundaries of orthodoxy. Attuned to the impossible hidden within the possible, mystical consciousness exceeds religion's stated boundaries to break into the hidden ground of love or into the mystery beneath the surface of convention. The mystics travel within this transgressive exceeding of borders without necessarily giving up their named religion (but sometimes that, too), primarily because they have become adept in transgression, in passing back and forth between living and dying, sight and blindness, knowing and unknowing.

The structure of these transgressive movements in and out of religion is experientially similar, if not the same. Our inborn capacity to be made empty, to partake of dying without death, opens the aperture of our souls or hearts, allowing us glimpses of the magnificence and magnitude of the holy. Even when we dream about a name or a beloved—Goddess, God, Ha-shem, Allah, Jesus—we are structurally bound to erasure and letting go. Face-to-face with God or Spirit, no name can be given or heard, no name can be rightfully claimed. As we pray to Durga or prostrate ourselves before Lord Buddha, we seek in the named ones our own unnaming, our own bridge to the ineffable. Is this not what Moses discovers on Mount Sinai when he asks of God, "What is your name?" The answer he receives—"I am what I am or I will be what I will be" (Ex. 3:13-14)—is not a name but passion, the totality of an excessive presence that sweeps us away, drawing us into a torrent of desire, taking away our breath and our words. Language, like our hearts, is wounded by the immeasurable, which pours forth more like tears of fire than any word we know. For the mystic temperament, in adoration of and longing for divine names, realizes the existential commitment to humility that inhabits every vision and every text. Even when St. Francis sings a hymn of praise to Brother Sun and Sister Moon, or Lao Tzu evokes the Tao, even then—and perhaps more so—in naming, the transgression of naming is at play. Always, and in every way, coming and going, contradiction and clarity, openness and closure move together, marking the text and exposing our hearts.

If we stop along the way to praise the gifts of presence—divine or otherwise—it is because we are called even then to the limitless movement of exceeding and being exceeded by what is presently possible. More often than not, even a fleeting glimpse of the holy is enough to imprint a photo negative in one's soul so that it can be recalled and reproduced over and again without so much as having to put a penny in the slot. Freely given, divinity cannot be bought or sold and, having etched a trace in our beings, serves as a reminder that the unrepresentable is never far away, always exceeding the limits of every identity. The name of God is always pointing toward this internalized emptying of self, this passion to be open to the cosmos, to the future, and to the freedom from knowing "I exist." As we swim in the ocean of formlessness, enlightenment is just another way of saying, *true feeling, true dying, true loving.*

Whether the mystic discovers a personal or impersonal reality, the deep self is flooded with a benevolent and a loving power, such that the heart is torn or wounded by an immense yearning nowhere assuaged. Having experienced alienation and aloneness, the mystic in us feels this aching benevolence and sweet tenderness of God and suffers over their absence and loss. I know of no permanent mystic flight to some realm of equanimity perpetually beyond the travesties and simple joys of life. Instead, the mystical dimension of consciousness sinks down into the world to be engaged by the daily moments that make up *now* and demands a reckoning with all that we give and receive. The dawning heart within each of us—the heart that is pure spirit—yearns for a moment of selflessness, for a spiritual love without self-interest. Here is where the mystic sight impregnates our bodies and leaves us without a home, for pathos has nowhere to rest its head, except in the arms of every other who is abandoned by the side of the road.

Mysticism scandalizes our complacency. It permits us to wake up, to open the eyes of the soul, and to proclaim the right to be fully aware of the great gift and burden placed upon us. In writing this extended discussion, my intention is neither to glorify nor generalize the "mystic" or the "mystical" as an individualized, personal experience separate from the fate of creation as a whole. Although clearly mysticism is tied to what we call by various names "the self," my task is different. It is to explore the contours of this new mystical consciousness that is working itself out not in boardrooms or clerical tribunals, but in the hearts and souls of individual seekers and the communities of faith they form.

Chapter FOUR

One without Name

When the *Apollo 14* mission launched into outer space on February 9, 1971, the astronauts on board were prepared for everything perhaps but the emotional impact of viewing how small and vulnerable is our planet. Glancing down on Earth, they discovered a new reverence for its nameless beauty and fragility and felt a visceral connection to life itself. Gone were the boundaries between peoples and nations; gone were the divisions of race and creed. Floating in the darkness of space was a sphere of brilliant deep blue oceans bordered by vibrant greens and dusty browns. Edgar Mitchell, one of the astronauts on board, described it this way:

> Suddenly, from behind the rim of the moon, in long, slow-motion moments of immense majesty, there emerges a sparkling blue and white jewel, a light, delicate sky-blue sphere laced with slowly swirling

veils of white, rising gradually like a small pearl in
a thick sea of black mystery. It takes more than a
moment to fully realize this is Earth . . . home. My
view of our planet was a glimpse of divinity.[1]

The impact of seeing the earth as an integral whole co-
extensive with the larger cosmos exerted a positive influence
on humanity's self-perception. It also became a culminating
symbol of the interdependence among nations, cultures, religions, and the biosphere that marks one of the most important insights of the twentieth century. In religious circles this
interdependence is furthered through dialogue among representatives of churches, mosques, synagogues, and sanghas who
encourage openness to each other's faiths and develop cooperative efforts toward alleviating human suffering. Monastic and
contemplative lineages also make significant contributions to
interreligious dialogue and the search for a common spirituality. The fruits of these encounters has led to a sense of global
responsibility for the earth as a whole and a commitment to a
new vision of right human and planetary relations.

At the same time large social, economic, and religious
forces advance the mutual relatedness of the global community,
a parallel process is taking place in the inner life of the person. Members of diverse religious traditions, as well as people
who claim no religious affiliation or belief, are aware of and
committed to interreligious dialogue as an essential dimension of world peace. They recognize in the external works of
greater understanding and cooperation among religions an
interior work of spiritual unity taking place in the depth of
their souls. Today's religious seekers find in the call to discover
the spiritual foundations of our common humanity a need to

find in oneself the inner peace that helps heal the fractures and violence within our world. In practicing this interior integration, spiritually attuned people realize it is truly not possible to conceive of the individual spiritual life in isolation from the fortunes and fates of creation as a whole. This reciprocal relationship between the dialogue of world religions, the inner life of the person, the fate of the earth, and the transcendent aspects of the human spirit is leading people today to a new revelatory vision based on the awareness of the common spirituality that binds us into one earth community.

Often without conscious awareness of the tremendous efforts made toward advancing religious cooperation, people find themselves called to search for and practice a spirituality inclusive of all life. Many, without benefit of study or community, have felt an interior longing to honor and practice the unity of creation. If the dialogue of traditions and cultures is in the vanguard of this advent of new religious paradigms, it is more than the creation and fostering of right human relations but also represents a search for the ontological roots of human religiosity. Exerting powerful influences on the spiritual integrity of the individual, such dialogue leads beyond appreciation for and cooperation with each other's traditions to a fundamental investigation of universal themes in a unitary light: nature of the self, divinity and humanity, sin and redemption, and social justice and human suffering.

I

> *Rise up nimbly and go on your strange journey*
> *to the ocean of meanings where you become one*
> *of those.*[2]
> ౨—୧ Rumi

Charlie sees me for spiritual direction once every month or two. He is a Catholic convert and a former Presbyterian elder. In one of our first sessions, he confided that his decision to explore other denominations was instigated by an urgent need for a more spiritual focus to his life. On a trip to Rome, the intensity of emotion he felt in St. Peter's Basilica ignited a hidden adoration in his heart he had not previously known. Traveling to Assisi and then Siena, he discovered in the lives of St. Francis and St. Catherine solace for his soul. For a number of years, there was peace in finding a new religious home. However, seven years later, and shortly before I first met him, Charlie began to realize that his identity within a Catholic context also has its oppressive elements. He worries about his dissatisfaction with a church culture that is increasingly insular and controlling of his time. He struggles with his conflict over attending mass and the subtle (and not so subtle) signals he receives from his faith community to believe and behave in a certain way. He wonders if his need for solitude and his negative gut reaction to formal prayers and religious socials are signs of pride or spiritual temerity.

Increasingly, Charlie finds meaning in the radical theology of Meister Eckhart and the spiritual practices of Zen. He is instinctively drawn toward a deep spiritual curiosity and an intensity of desire to know God outside limitations of religion, gender, or culture. He finds himself traveling on the many roads offered by the world's religions, incorporating elements of Hindu worship, Sufi prayers, and Native American shamanism in his daily life and work. Even as Charlie's heart expands through the mysterious workings of spirit, he continues to question his loyalties and the impasse between his Christian commitment and the spiritual openness to which he is drawn. He asks: "Is this movement within my deepest self an authentic path initiated by the Divine, or is it some self-absorbed foray into sin and betrayal? How can I tell? How can I know?"

In my practice of spiritual direction and in my faculty role, I have heard hundreds of stories like Charlie's. There is a new spiritual movement afoot, initiated not by religions or masters, but by the action of the Divine in the souls of people around the globe. It is a direct touching of the inner spark of the soul by divine mystery that is calling people—many of whom never thought about leaving their tradition—to a deeper experience of the sacred that is related to but outside of formal religious community. While individual in the context of life experience, this global spiritual movement shares certain common characteristics that herald the unfolding of a new revelatory consciousness for humanity. In naming it "revelatory," my intention is to emphasize that this multireligious spiritual focus is not something constructed by people to assuage religious doubt and confusion or to be rebellious and prideful. Rather, it emerges as a faith experience of the utmost seriousness that compels each person to give up whatever is oppressive, superior, exclusive, hurtful, or violent in his or her own religious worldview. It is felt as a deep compunction in the soul to dispense with religious sectarianism, pride, or possessiveness. Sometimes such life-changing transformations occur in a torrent of illumination. More often, realization is arrived at through struggle, suffering, and pain.

People from all stations of life and religious traditions find themselves grappling with questions similar to the ones Charlie raises. They live today in a spiritual paradox, between paradigms, if you will, neither comfortable with their historical tradition (if they have one), nor fully aware of the spiritual implications of the rumblings and musings of their hearts. I have witnessed the challenges contemporary pilgrims confront as they struggle in silence and obedience on the narrow and often winding path of a new faith journey. Whether they follow a spiritual path within a tradition or are outside tradition without the comfort of belonging to a community of believers, they often trek alone and without support into the metaphorical desert to grow closer to God. Among the more ardent of these seekers are those who have studied many of the world's religions and gleaned from them meaning, direction, and wisdom.

These sojourners are not alone in having a faith or practicing a spirituality without religion. I find there is an increasingly large group of people who seek meaning and comfort on the edges and outside the boundaries of the denominational traditions. According to recent statistics, the number of Americans who claim no religious affiliation or self-identify as multireligious, interreligious, spiritual but not religious, or New Age, has doubled in the last ten years to an estimated 29 million. Social scientists and other chroniclers of popular culture term these individuals "unaffiliated," with the implication that they profess to belong to no organized religion or faith tradition. But to be unaffiliated with a religion does not translate to "no belief." The vast majority of those who claim no religious sect believe in a higher power, supreme being, or God. In their diverse spiritual expressions—from yoga, to nature walks, to Kabbalah study, to Goddess worship—the religiously eclectic are changing the landscape of faith.[3]

It is not solely the unavowed among us who heed the call of religious openness and spiritual unity. Our neighbors and friends who belong to religious denominations also struggle to find spiritual companions who share their feelings of openness to and respect for other religions or even a lonely traveler of like mind. I meet individuals who are torn by the same concerns Charlie brings to our spiritual direction sessions. Devoted to their religion, they are troubled by the exclusiveness or superiority demanded by their denomination, and live an uneasy relationship with glaring moral questions and social doctrines that are at odds with their deepest beliefs. Others, committed to the formal expression of their Buddhist, Greek Orthodox, Lutheran, or Reform Jewish congregation, nonetheless feel religious exclusivity is contrary to their faith. For these and other reasons, some people have left their religion of birth to convert to another tradition, while others consider themselves to be multireligious—Jewish and Buddhist, Christian and Hindu, Quaker-Catholic-Buddhist, Native American-Goddess-Lutheran—participating in the rituals and living the tenets of more than one faith tradition. Still others may be agnostic or atheistic in their orientation but, nonetheless, are moved by a religious sentiment, a longing for the *wholly other*.

This journey of openness to other religions or to a spiritual life without religion is born of prayers and tears. It is not a superficial entertainment or a naïve belief. Rather, it is a wounding felt deep within the self that calls into question and suffers over the violence of exclusion, indifference, superiority, injustice, and oppression—subtle and overt—that inhabits religions and turns the heart against itself. The call to mystical openness is echoed across millennia of humanity's wisdom; it is the call to discover the unitary point of view that holds the promise of a more just and peaceful planet. It is God's dark night in us, an impasse between spiritual paradigms that is leading us to a new and deeper understanding of the sacred and of our part in the transformation of the world. While religious authorities and institutional structures advance or impede its flow, the spirit comes in the silence of night to teach us in secret about love, true love, that knows no difference of creed.

In this pilgrimage, many are wandering in the desert for forty times forty long years, not sure where they are going or if they have arrived. It is often sparse and lonely. There are few signposts along the way, and the occasional traveler that one meets more often than not takes weary pilgrims for half-crazed don Quixotes on the prowl. It is not an easy road, this wandering away from the road maps and grocery stores of the organized religions. There is always the temptation to tame it and make it palatable to the ardent criticisms that come one's way: this is not a real religion, it is only New Age spirituality, Goddess worship, or a pluralistic smorgasbord of tasty bites from many religions. This path has no authenticity; it traces its lineage back to no certifiable prophet, messiah, or guru. Who could believe it? Who would follow it? There is even the prohibition, mentioned in the back rooms of interreligious dialogue conferences, that only those who come with a determinate faith are allowed into the discussion of interfaith. One must have a named faith—a certifiable faith—to enter the circle of dialogue. Those who do not are kept away from the table and perhaps diminished or ridiculed for their inability to find words to say they have a religion without religion or a God with no name.

The common ground among these various pilgrims is threefold: (1) they uphold what Mahatma Gandhi called "the manyness of truth" and are uncomfortable with religious languages and liturgical forms that exclude, oppress, or patronize; (2) they are following an authentic spiritual path—often in the dark and without spiritual languages or community support—to what impassions them, to what calls them in the depth of their souls; and (3) in the process, they are giving life to a new lineage of religious truths, to the deep structure of the religious itself, before it is formalized and takes a name—before it is co-opted and saddled with the dogmatism of the religious "ought."

In the hearts and minds of these modern sojourners, the gestation of new spiritual traditions is taking place, born of the personal yearning and intuitive wisdom of those who have dared to follow the call. This distinctive spiritual journey, which affirms the unity of existence and the universality of faith, is leading us to a new global consciousness and the development of what is alternately termed an interfaith, interspiritual, or interreligious contemplative practice. It is the discovery of a oneness greater than our differences and a common spirituality that heals the divide in human consciousness and, by so doing, provides the sacred foundation for a global culture.

II

> *According to the Talmud, the Sabbath is me'en 'olam ha-ba, which means: somewhat like eternity or the world to come.*[4]
> — Abraham Joshua Heschel

On a subsequent visit, Charlie brings several books he has been reading to our session. Jumping right into what has been stirring up his thoughts, he wants to discuss Heschel's idea that paradise or the world to come is in our midst. Pulling from his briefcase an outline he created the previous evening, Charlie tells me about the distress he feels on a daily basis that he is not living a more spiritual life. He talks about his commitment to meditation and spiritual reading. He tries to attend Mass on Sunday, but some weeks he just cannot get himself to go. He feels some progress in his prayer life and finds the moments of quiet growing within him. Presently, he is studying the thought of the Jewish mystic Abraham Heschel and of the Catholic saint, St. John of the Cross. Both Heschel and John wrote out of an eternity present in the now, even as they suffered the fate of society's ignorance and prejudice. Through them, Charlie hopes to feel closer to God in his daily life, although he still feels stunted by an inability to make sense of the inner conflict he feels. He recounts a dream where he is inside the cell of John of the Cross, imprisoned by his own friars. In the dark shadows of this tiniest of spaces, a supernatural light shines on John's bowed head. I ask, "How does this dream relate to what you are going through in your spiritual life?"

This question breaks a logjam inside Charlie. He tells me how dry and unsettling his inner life feels. He prays God is close because he feels *nothing*. Trying to hold on to his inner anguish long enough to make words, Charlie says he cannot force himself to be a committed Catholic or an unbeliever. Last week Father Daniel, his parish priest, officiated at a close friend's wedding and announced to the congregation that only baptized Catholics were invited to receive the Eucharist. He says that "made me crazy." His wife, Eleanor, was also offended, because the entire service referred to God as "he." "I'm broken up inside," Charlie tells me. "Nothing is the same anymore. I'm behind bars, brought to my knees by my own community. I see the Light shining on me, but I don't know how to open the locked cell."

Spiritual direction is about these sorts of issues. In times past, Chinese sages, Indian gurus, and other spiritual directors have heard stories relevant to their own times and cultures, but I believe the Charlies of today encounter a unique set of soul dilemmas. Not only are they working through the normal issues that affect every spiritual life—absence of God, appropriate spiritual decision making, or prayer practice—they also confront soul questions specific to living both within a formed spiritual universe and one that is still being born.

I suspect that Buddha's followers worked through their own conflicts over Hinduism and their new faith, as did Jews who were also Christians in the early centuries of the church. Since much of what transpires within a spiritual direction context is transmitted from heart to heart, these important faith discussions are seldom in the public domain. Charlie reminds me that our contemporary world needs a spiritual foundation adequate to the pressing moral, religious, economic, and social inequities affecting our souls. His pain reinforces my intention to empower others to become spiritually literate in the language structures and ways of knowing that allow us to speak about what has been unspoken and to name what has remained unnamed. Charlie's reaction to the officiating priest at his friend's wedding emphasizes how urgent is our need to find a way to evaluate and interpret our common humanity and our shared earthly concerns in a manner respectful and inclusive of our differences.

While the wisdom of the world's religious lineages are essential to the task, they are not alone—or even together— sufficient. What is needed is a new thinking of the religious and a more radical expression of the mystical that begins from a premise never before considered on a global scale. We need a spirituality profoundly respectful of humanity's diverse participation in the sacred, that is also unifying and humble, rooted in the earth, sustained by the diversity of life forms, and respectful of the emerging wisdom traditions, among them the ecological, liberationist, feminist, third world, and interreligious.

We need a shared spiritual vision able to address our universe and humanity's place in it as an integrated whole. From the smallest subatomic particle to the movement of mass objects in space, life itself operates on principles best described as integral and holistic, unified and universal. While we may not yet have the instruments—both mental and technological—to measure or understand all the subtle processes that animate the cosmos, we have been traveling over these last several centuries on a path toward greater unification of theory and experience. While our technology has enabled us to glimpse the earth from the perspective of outer space, mystics throughout history have mapped inner space, a space both dependent upon and moving toward an integral unity. Despite the horrible wars that have scarred our planetary home and the continued racking pain that threatens to bring us to the brink of despair, the blood of oneness pulsates through our veins like the power of a religious conviction, connecting us in spite of our troubled history to a source of communion too profound and breath-taking to ignore. If we are able to deny the intrinsic interdependence of life, it is only because our natural and instinctive mystical awareness has succumbed to a rationalist mind-set and is thus undeveloped, ridiculed, or ignored.

Renowned Muslim scholar and mystic Louis Massignon called this all-encompassing reality *le point vierge* ("the virgin point") to signify the "mystic's deep knowledge of God . . . and the secret center of the heart."[5] Later adopted by Thomas Merton, *le point vierge* came to represent for him "a point of nothingness [at the center of our being] which is untouched by sin and by illusion, a point of pure truth, a point or spark that belongs entirely to God."[6] Both interior and exterior to the self, the unity of existence in our own secret center provides a global paradigm for human and planetary sustainability. It does not need to be invented as it is already within us—we are made of and by unity—and no doubt it is already unfolding. It is certainly most completely expressed in the teachings of the seers and saints, whose collective thought forms one of the most sustained meditations on the oneness of existence. For it seems that from whichever corner of the globe, or whatever religious persuasion, the mystic voice speaks out of an integral unity, totally present everywhere without division.

Experience has taught me that Charlie will not abandon his Christian heritage. Rather, he will find within the Christian mysteries the point of nothingness that breaks the bounds of specific religious forms and opens his heart to the holy. He also will find compassion for Father Daniel who no doubt is trying to stem the tide of a spiritual uprising growing outside religion, which is pouring into our communities and confounding religious leaders who wonder what can be done to return their flocks to the fold. Instead, the religiously unaffiliated—and those who are within tradition but wounded by the exclusive or separatist—are heeding the call of a deeper faith, a new vision of the world as truly integral and whole. More important, Charlie will accept and be comforted by the fact that this common spirituality is not against or instead of, but in addition to, his Christian faith. Religious openness does not require us to leave behind our love for our own savior, messiah, bodhisattva, prophet, or god. Rather, we are called to witness the unifying stream that runs like a deep current within each of us, and to harness the power of these streams until a mighty river of compassion floods our world with love.

Yes, our common spirituality may be seen by some people as a new religious movement that is striking out into the desert to grow closer to the holy. But if it is a religion, it is unlike any we have known, for it is free of the universalist or exclusivist claim and without need of a determinate form or final name. Its underlying structure is dynamic and self-emptying, radically democratic and absent of one all-inspiring prophet. Divinity is breaking into our souls, challenging our understanding of religion and radicalizing our claim on the revelatory. The Holy comes to each of us singularly, pouring into the inner point of stillness where the nothingness of self meets the nothingness of God. Through the force of a nameless and faceless moral persuasion, we are obligated to root out the hidden veins of exclusiveness and potential violence that still grip our hearts. From some depth of our own souls, we are called to question how our religious identity contributes to or endorses suffering and pain, as we are invited to stand up for nonviolence and "nonharm."

In these various expressions, we operate from a deeper feeling, practicing in our hearts and living out on the ground a common spirituality, which, like the great mother river Ganges, flows through everything, watering and nourishing our souls. Many of the spiritual giants of these last centuries have written and lived this common spirituality. We are not alone. I am reminded of the poem by the esteemed fourteenth-century Sufi mystic and theologian Ibn al' Arabi, which expresses a theme common to the life and thought of modern saints.

> O Marvel! a garden amidst the flames.
> My heart has become capable of every form:
> it is a pasture for gazelles and a
> convent for Christian monks,
> and a temple for idols and the pilgrim's Kaa'ba,
> and the tables of the Torah and the book of the
>   Qu'ran.
> I follow the religion of Love:
> whatever way Love's camels take,
> that is my religion and my faith.[7]

The Shaykh's celebration of all paths to Truth is shared by many of the great thinkers of the most recent centuries. In the midst of human atrocity and indifference—Abraham Heschel's narrow escape from Auschwitz; Howard Thurman's mystical insight into the suffering of Black Americans; Dorothy Day's solidarity with political dissidents and the indignities heaped on the working poor; Thich Nhat Hahn's witness to the grim tragedy of Vietnam—they found peace, a door into a new world, a vision of another reality, the proof that an invisible but tangible presence of love courses through the veins of history. Heralding the arrival of a new or deeper spirituality, they found a contemplative religion within their own tradition that was greater than the practices of their day. They lived at a level that impelled and commanded them to be prophetic voices for a new kind of human society, one that was broadly global, pluralistic, and inclusive of multiple perspectives, religions, cultures, and ideas. Rather than their vision being diffuse or marginalized, it was instead central to their faith: greater than religion is God; more profound than words is silence; deeper than division and conflict is mercy and peace.

None of these people were shielded from the pains and sufferings of everyday life; none of them preached—even those like Thomas Merton who was physically cloistered—in a vacuum; none of them sought an easy way out, shortcut, or detour around the conflicts and confusions of daily life. Instead, their vision and their practice arose from an indelible faith, sustained by their religion of birth, but widely expanded until it included the whole world and all religions. It was a faith born out of suffering that understood completely and profoundly that all creation is loved. This love was so fierce, so present, so expansive, and so passionate that to deny it or to reject it became an impossibility.

Equally, these people of wisdom were concerned that we not succumb to despair, loss of hope, or self-betrayal. They knew that only the spirit can provide us with the necessary strength to suffer through defeat and continue to strive for victory. But what a strange victory they sought. It was not one of power or control, but a victory over the human heart, over all that is narrow, violent, exclusive, demeaning, or raw. Each, in her or his own way, practiced what could be called a contemplative religion—that is, they were prophets who found their way in a common stream of reality that flows through all religions. They had become universal in their particularity and vessels of mercy for all of life. Their very presence engenders great respect—these women and men who lived on the borders of a new country, where there truly is a new way of being human.

III

She is ineffable sweetness, Radha-Krishna the love play that dissolves conventionality. She is Sita-Rom, compassionately wise, the complete evolution of humanity.[8]
 —ᴄᴄ Ramakrishna

A few months later Charlie came for spiritual direction again. He spent a week at a Carmelite woman's monastery in silence and, miraculously, has started to feel the impasse inside him breaking up. He consciously recognizes the birth pangs of a new spiritual life taking up residence in his body and his soul. This conversion comes in a way that is so subtle and gentle that his old ways of understanding and evaluation are too clumsy or coarse to recognize, let alone speak, its immensity. While away he had a vision of the Divine Mother kneeling in front of a statue of Mary in the woods. He describes the mothering and nurturing energy that fills his soul as a feeling so tender and merciful that he can barely understand what she is. She pours into him, filling him with an adoration that he had learned to suppress, and society often ridicules and shames. Charlie gathers her perfume, bathing his weary soul in her fragrant light. He feels her gentle touch flowing through him, like mercy healing pain. Every religious sentiment he ever had is contained within her, illuminating creation's beauty and anointing him with unifying light.

The fact that none of us can identify or name this new revealing consciousness—or own or consume it—is the sign of her holy presence. She is here all around us. Distinct from the emergence of many prior shifts in planetary history, this new realization of the Divine Feminine is not presenting itself only through one seer or prophet, or one female or male messiah or lord. Rather, having traced an inscription in our hearts of something more elusive and intangible, her seeds are being sowed in the depth of our own wholeness and are germinating now into a collective and interdependent spiritual journey unlike any in recorded history. It is as if the wisdom of all the ancients and the vision of all our futures have come together to give birth to offspring who are already undivided in their source.

We cannot find what we seek by the old expansionist methods. We are not enlightened by virtue of giving over our identities for an undisclosed future, but by following the passion gnawing in our guts to leave behind that which can be distinguished or claimed. We are called into the existential desert, a desert that looks a bit different today than it did to our monastic forebears, a desert that is difficult to inhabit with any regularity amid the noise and busyness of daily life. This movement into the desert is not a journey, actually; not a striking out to foreign shores or starry heavens, although these too have their place. Rather, the radical wisdom that is the mark of solitary places reveals itself and is discovered in the commitment to sink down into the place we inhabit, like brother Benedict and his cenobitic band of monks. In turning our attention to the spirit's flourishing on earth, we learn how to celebrate and sustain the divine consciousness of the future being born now. Through accepting responsibility for our embodiment, and for the ordinary events that give life meaning, we glimpse the habitation of the sacred within our midst. And somehow, in the throes of everything else, comes a spiritual belonging that feels at home everywhere but resides nowhere. It lays down before us an invisible blanket of meaning that imposes nothing but informs everything.

It is almost like saying if we were to achieve the enlightenment or salvation prescribed by all our religions—rather than imagining this in some realm after death, in some heaven away from home—we would come back to *this world* ready to work together in the essential wisdom that underlies every religious sentiment: *Let it be on earth as it is in heaven.* Global spirituality begins not from the journey toward enlightenment or salvation, but it begins in and through an enlightened, saving perspective. It asks and compels us to leap into an illumined state of awareness, to sink down into the present that is also the *eternal now* in order to commit ourselves to the task of lifting the world up to its sacred potential.

Our civilizations and religions have been so directed toward the other world, another truth, a heaven beyond, that we have left the holiness of the present to those perhaps least capable among us to guide us into a new future. When I reflect on Charlie, I am more convinced than ever that we need to discover and enact an impossible hope that already dwells among us, without waiting for the "to come" and the "not-yet." By seizing what is now present with all of our strength and determination and raising it up to its own luminosity, we plant the seeds of the future. We have ignored the sacredness of this world, having given up and given over hope that we can ever be more than "merely" human. Now is our time to be unveiled, to offer ourselves to silence, and to become votaries of peace, forging a global community where none are excluded and all are welcomed to the table of communion. Now is our time to follow the precepts and the sacrifices made by our prophetic ancestors, those men and women who dwelled in the heart of reality where love (is all there) is.

Chapter FIVE

In Search of Common Ground

As a young seminarian, Ewert Cousins volunteered to work on the Rosebud Reservation in South Dakota. Having entered the Jesuit Seminary at eighteen, he was deeply rooted in Ignatian spirituality and now, more than twelve years later, was only months away from ordination. Perhaps it was something about the stark blue sky of the upper plains or the roping of cattle as he followed Chief Hollow Horn Bear through the high sage brush; maybe it was the way the air filled his lungs and the great cumulous clouds cast shadows over his soul; or maybe it was the loosening of ties and the breath of fresh air that allowed his heart to be pierced by another way of being. Whatever it was, something happened to Ewert Cousins on the Rosebud reservation, something that changed the course of his life's work.

He tells us today that he was suddenly aware that the Brulé Lakota with whom he was living had a profound spirituality and an understanding of sacramentality that was distinct from the Catholicism of his youth. He discovered an immense value in their love of the land and organic harmony with nature, as well as their dynamic understanding of time and their immersion in myth and ritual. Cousins recognized that without ascribing to the spiritual tenets that anchored his faith—Trinity, Jesus, Eucharist—the Lakota Sioux lived and practiced a holy life. He somehow realized there and then that he had crossed over into another world—a world of open possibility and immense hope—and had come back a different man:

> I vividly remember the day, while I was talking to a group of Lakota, that I felt my consciousness, as it were, extend itself out of my body and pass over into their consciousness. From that moment I felt I could see things from their perspective and experience their values from within their world. Also I could look back at my own world and see its values in a clearer light— but also its limitations![1]

These events proved decisive personally and academically. Not long after, Ewert Cousins left the Jesuit seminary, without abandoning his religion of birth, to devote his life to scholarly and spiritual study on the dialogue of the world's religions. Fascinated by his experience of entering into the spiritual universe of another culture, Cousins recognized that he had come into contact with the "essence of dialogic consciousness."[2] More than a personal encounter, his ability to pass over into other worldviews and come back with new insight demonstrated to him that dialogic consciousness was not confined to personal instances and experiences, but reflected a new universe of understanding.

I

I came to the conclusion long ago, after
prayerful search and study, that all religions
were true, and also that all had some error in
them, and whilst I hold my own, I should hold
others as dear.[3]

ᗩ—ᕉ Mohandas K. Gandhi

Cousins's conversion from a focus on religion to an open embrace of all genuine faith experiences traces a pattern followed by other pioneers in the history and psychology of religion. Over this last century and a half, individuals from diverse religious backgrounds and intellectual communities have discovered in their own spirit a doorway into a vast open terrain. We can trace some of these beginnings to the mid-nineteenth century and the scholarship of the European philosophical school known as *Religionswissenschaft*, or history of religions. Steeped in the scientific mind-set that pervaded the period—bounded on one side by the dusk of the Enlightenment and on the other by the dawn of Darwinism—historians of religions were intent on the discovery of a common core to the human religious quest. Two distinguishing features of this early research were a shared concern to study religion scientifically in a manner free from the doctrinal claims of a specific tradition and to seek for what is universal and common in the human spiritual quest.

Released from the constraints of religious dogma, scholars sought a broader, more inclusive interpretation of religious consciousness. Since historians of religions presumed that reason or science could never lay claim to understanding faith or theology, they turned instead to the external rituals and practices of religious expression in the hope that through careful and painstaking analysis the underlying universal religion would be uncovered. Much as an archaeologist pieces together the fragments of a civilization to reconstruct the original whole, so did scholars of comparative religion hope that by fitting together the puzzles of many and diverse traditions they would uncover the original religion of which each particular religion was a significant, but fragmentary, part. These pioneers of what might be called a modern religious worldview were seeking to be objective observers of the religious dimension of life without allowing confessions of faith to intrude.

Around the same time, other scholars, among them Rudolf Otto, William James, and Evelyn Underhill, specifically included religious experience in comparative study and provided groundbreaking documentation of the significance of faith in human development. Their efforts provided a philosophical background for the development of interreligious dialogue that would ensue over the next one hundred years. In their respective landmark studies, Otto (*The Idea of the Holy*), James (*Varieties of Religious Experience*), and Underhill (*Mysticism*) were concerned with the dynamics of religious experience, especially mystical or spiritual states, and their validity as important sources of knowledge and meaning.

Otto's work emphasized the universal characteristics associated with transcendent experiences of the sacred, while James's main intention was to document and analyze instances of genuine religious events and thus refute the medical reductionism that relegated altered states of consciousness to physiological epiphenomena. Underhill undertook a similarly ambitious project in developing an enduring body of work on mystical traditions and stages of spiritual development. In each of these studies, religious experience was established as an integral dimension of the person, and its validity as a central element in cultural analysis was emphasized.

These individuals bequeathed to future generations questions of immense importance. For one, they broke the stranglehold that religion, especially their own Christian religion, exerted over free inquiry and empirical research. In the process, they unraveled the strands of denominational faiths from the religious dimension of consciousness intrinsic to all humans. By turning the methods of science and the social sciences toward the structure of religion itself, they generated not only a new kind of public inquiry, but also a new dimension of critical awareness. Their efforts have allowed us to gaze across the landscape of religious consciousness over diverse historical periods, cultural contexts, and geographical locations. For the first time, we are able to view the development of the human spiritual quest as an integrated whole.

II

> *In every corner of my soul exists an altar to a different god.*[4]
>
> ℔—℗ Fernando Pessoa

The contemporary discipline of interreligious, interfaith dialogue owes a great debt of gratitude to the history of religions and to the critical studies of mystical states undertaken by Otto, James, and Underhill. It also is enriched by the formative contributions of Aldous Huxley, Pierre Teilhard de Chardin, Gershom Scholem, Henri Corbin, D. T. Suzuki, Mircea Eliade, and Raimon Panikkar, to name a few. Certainly without such comparative study there would be no intellectual foundation for addressing the complexity of issues raised by competing truth claims and religious communities.

Along with these academic pursuits, interreligious dialogue was supported by burgeoning movements led by both practitioners and representatives of the world's traditions. The first modern attempt at religious convergence was the Parliament of the World's Religions, which brought spiritual leaders from around the globe to Chicago in 1893. The World Missionary Conference of Edinburgh in 1910, the establishment in 1948 of the World Council of Churches, and Vatican II (1962–65), respectively, opened the floodgates for dialogue between Christians and members of other religious traditions. While each of these efforts understandably had an intra-Christian focus, they also included and developed important subcommittees and outreach efforts aimed at developing respect and cooperation among the world's religions.

The words "interreligious," "interfaith," "ecumenical," and "interideological" are used interchangeably within the academy, as well as in pastoral settings and the media, to express the coming together of two or more denominations, religious traditions, or ideological positions for the purpose of greater understanding and cooperation. The term "interreligious dialogue" most frequently refers to the exchange of theologies, beliefs, ceremonies, and cooperative work for social justice among representatives of the world's religions. The concept of "interfaith dialogue," on the other hand, tends to emphasize the sharing of personal and communal religious experiences, including specific faith dimensions, inner motivations, spiritual practices, and ritual expressions across traditions.

While "ecumenical" is an adjective meaning "universal"—derived from the Greek word *oikoumene*, "the inhabited world" or "the whole world"—it has been adopted (some say co-opted) by Christians to express relations between and among Christian denominations. It also, however, can denote the relationship between different religious traditions, for all traditions are part of the "inhabited world." Religions today also find themselves in frequent "interideological" conversation with political, economic, and cultural ideologies. Lately, more people use the term "interfaith" as a noun, rather than an adjective, to underscore that their faith commitment or religion *is* interreligious.

Contemporary interreligious dialogue has come to challenge the methods, theories of knowing, and interpretive frameworks adopted from the history of religions. In general, participants in interreligious exchanges find the social scientific approach to faith and religious experiences to be inadequate in explaining the complexities of humanity's cross-cultural religious heritage. Of equal concern is the imposition of Western metaphysics and cosmologies on other world traditions and the destructive potential that religious imperialism exerts on the spiritual integrity of peoples and cultures. Confronted with diverse and often competing philosophies, cosmologies, and metaphysics, interreligious partners search for a language to express both the variety of humanity's religious legacy and the underlying unity to which pluralism attests. Interreligious dialogue seeks to define, identify, and systematize a previously unknown capacity of human awareness: the *collective discernment* of a common spiritual matrix to human life.

III

> *In dialogue, each partner must listen to the other as openly and sympathetically as possible.*[5]
> ⟶ Leonard Swidler

One of the more transformative courses I have taught is the "History and Theology of Interreligious Dialogue." Students tell me it is personally empowering for them to study the background and philosophy behind contemporary religious cooperation. They learn that interreligious dialogue has been integral to the development of all the world religions, although its present evolution has far broader implications than what has come before.

Today, formal dialogue among religions is self-consciously committed to four areas: (1) the importance of personal faith experience as a foundation for authentic dialogue; (2) the communal discernment of truth as a necessary element in clarifying the truth claims of one's own tradition; (3) the discovery of alternative modes of knowing and methods of interpretation that affirm the unitive, mystical, and nondual aspects of consciousness; and (4) the emergence of new visions of reality and new revelations found through contemplative awareness, dialogue, and exploration.

Religious Experience. Seminary students bring with them their religious wounds and their spiritual triumphs. Rebecca, a physician who views her medical practice as a form of ministry, entered the interfaith ordination program because she felt God was calling her to the path of spiritual nonviolence. Raised in an orthodox Jewish family, she was under constant pressure in medical school to find a way to negotiate her family's religious practices with her secular education. Offered a research fellowship to study causes of blindness in Thailand, her initial trepidation at leaving Brooklyn was soon displaced by friendships with Christian missionaries and Buddhist monks working alongside her in the villages. Her initiation into interreligious dialogue started with morning visits to Buddhist temples and continued during those nights when she discussed religious experiences over dinner with her new Mennonite friends.

Profoundly touched by the devotional spirit of the Thai people, Rebecca's clinical work brought her into contact with many faith traditions, including a community of Franciscan sisters. Invited to attend a silent retreat, Rebecca discovered that she was surprisingly open to monasticism and the liturgy of the hours. She was even more amazed that her fear of somehow betraying her family's faith was, instead, replaced by a deeper appreciation for Judaism. It was during her travels in Asia that she began to have intense feelings of longing for God and the beginnings of an inchoate faith yearning to be recognized and named.

Indeed, personal religious experience is a primary criterion for authentic dialogue. Without it, Rebecca found that it is impossible to truly understand another person's religion from inside his or her experience. When the personal component is absent—when each partner is unwilling to be open and discuss his or her inner life—dialogue is not transformative or illuminating. Rather, it runs the risk of getting bogged down in intellectual debate or religious posturing. By creating an environment conducive to sharing experiences of faith, discussions are mutually respectful and more authentic. Through a sympathetic engagement with another person's devotion to the sacred, partners in dialogue learn more accurately and more profoundly about each other's traditions from *within*.

Raimon Panikkar speaks of understanding others from within when he says that "religious dialogue must proceed from the depths of my religious attitude to these same depths in my partner."[6] Of course, neither faith nor religious experience is confined to those who practice a religion. Rather, they represent constitutive dimensions of the person, and are the driving force behind the search for meaning and belonging that underlies all human quests. Faith and religious experience are expressed in the resolve, intrinsic to the human spirit, to move forward, to continue to say "yes" when we are confronted with illness, disappointment, pain, or doubt. The word "faith" in "interfaith" refers to the force within the human spirit that gives us the strength to be vulnerable and resilient in the face of life's tragedies and joys.

Entering Each Other's Truth. As Ewert Cousins experienced, to enter the sacred depths of another tradition and to understand it as his own, he had to cross over into the reality of the Lakota Sioux in mutual trust—not as stranger but as friend. He had to be free of coercion or justification of his Christian beliefs, be willing to accept his partners as equals, and be aware of any hidden sentiments toward the special nature of his own religious claims. Cousins discovered that this intimate sharing in the indigenous traditions of the Lakota necessarily led him to shed misinformation concerning his dialogue partners, discover spiritual wisdom and practices in their tradition that could enrich his own, and rethink religious categories and definitions in light of this shared communion.

Dialogic consciousness is rooted in one's own spirituality yet is openly receptive to the growth that takes place through an interpenetration of truths. Moreover, Cousins's experience showed him that this sharing of religious traditions is *necessary* for clarifying the truth claims of one's own tradition. In fact, many participants in dialogue believe that the ultimate validity of a religion's claim to uniqueness can *only* be known in dialogue with other traditions.

A practical example of such interreligious discernment is evident in the development of global ethics, human rights accords, and other theoretical questions that have a powerful impact on the world situation. The answer to compelling planetary issues—environmental degradation, violence, genocide, poverty, hunger—are not simply given in the scriptures and traditions of any one religion. Rather, the answers must be worked out through practical dialogue among representatives of the world's religions and secular philosophies in order to develop new solutions to current social problems.

These creative encounters with multiple spiritual worldviews lead to practical considerations concerning one's own faith. In internships at churches, synagogues, mosques, and sanghas, seminary students learn that dialogue is not aimed toward the assimilation or substitution of one tradition by another. Rather, true interest in another person's religion opens the self to the practice of peace. Most students find this practice, the spiritual commitment to nonviolence, to be one of the most personally challenging. Because genuine dialogue puts us in touch with our souls, it exposes the false self and the roots of separateness and conflict. We become aware as never before of the subtle feelings of superiority, anger, or contempt we harbor toward others who believe differently. In our hearts, we suffer from the violent ways we treat the spirit of life and the harshness we inflict on ourselves or others. Further, we admit the pain that offensive, sexist, or wrathful scriptural languages exert on our souls. For these reasons, interfaith seminarians find that the spirituality of nonviolence is one of the most powerful indicators of unresolved soul wounds. As nonviolence heightens our sensitivity to how we treat other people and religions, students discover the root basis of compassion and the fundamental benevolence of the spirit.

Alternative Ways of Knowing. The process Cousins calls "dialogic consciousness" raises an important question: how are we able to know and enter into the inner life of other traditions? John Dunne, in his book *The Way of All the Earth*, proposes the concept of "passing over." Using the powers of images and imagination, "passing over," he writes, "is a shifting in standpoint, a going over to the standpoint of another culture, another way of life, another religion. It is followed by an equal and opposite process we might call 'coming back,' coming back with new insight to one's own culture, one's own way of life, one's own religion."[7]

This is precisely how Cousins described his experience with the Lakota people. It is also how Rebecca recounted her ability to enter with her heart and soul into Buddhist meditation practices and into Christian monastic liturgies. She felt that she had discovered deep structures of reality common to all humans through a penetration into the sacred archetypes of these traditions. Once identified by her Jewish background and its ways of knowing and seeing, she now realized that inside herself she contained the capacity to leave "the confines of her own historical horizon and travel into the value-world of another tradition, returning with new spiritual insight and wisdom."[8]

Similarly, Rebecca was surprised at how her knowledge of these traditions came about through personal participation in interreligious dialogue and transcendent experiences. She saw that spiritual life is a series of interactive events that occurs in the context of her total life relationships. Deep communion can never be externally imposed, but is the result of the cocreation of spiritual worlds within one's own heart. Rebecca's experience at the Franciscan monastery, for example, involved her in an interactive "communion and co-creative participation" with Christian sacraments. Her individual consciousness did not appropriate, possess, or passively represent this knowledge but was infused with and intimately involved in Jewish and Christian spiritual worlds.[9]

Human beings are always swimming in the ocean of divinity. The very existence of the human person is a self-disclosure of spirit, and a window into the sacred. In Rebecca's interreligious journey, her spirit, and the spirits of others with whom she met and shared religious experiences, received another unveiling of Mystery. Dialogic consciousness, then, represents a cocreative participation in truth making. Truth is not already finalized "out there," but is creatively enacted and revealed in the process of sharing in and learning from another worldview or perspective—a process that leads to *new* visions of reality and *new* dimensions of consciousness not known before.

New Visions of Reality. Most striking to practitioners embarked on the interreligious spiritual quest is that they become more and more comfortable with paradox and uncertainty. As Rebecca and Ewert Cousins experienced, interreligious dialogue affirms the underlying common ground of spirituality and the oneness of the divine mystery. Yet it affirms this unity from the perspective of a radical openness that does not diminish, reduce, or homogenize the distinctiveness and beauty of their respective Jewish and Catholic backgrounds. Through bearing in themselves the "manyness" and oneness of the divine mystery, Rebecca and Ewert Cousins participated in new expressions and new understandings of reality not conceivable within one tradition alone. They found that dialogue itself becomes the medium of new revelatory dimensions or new spiritual paradigms. For each of them, the interreligious, interfaith journey led to a personal embodiment of and participation in global consciousness and holistic spiritual practices.

These compelling interreligious events are leading to a spiritual renaissance in which creative religious forms and styles of ministry are being developed. Having dispensed with the idea that one religion can be all in all, interreligious, interfaith dialogue provides a forum that invites spiritual pilgrims to sanctify and honor the indwelling of the sacred in their lives. Through multireligious rituals, liturgies, and prayer services, dialogue partners are immersed in the human spiritual quest and in the sacramental elements intrinsic to worship and prayer. At the same time, it is through this deepening awareness of global spiritual fellowship and responsibility that they find the courage to establish a theological imperative for planetary harmony based on the equality of persons, ethical concern for all creation, and the spirituality of the earth.

Interreligious dialogue calls for a recognition that all religions are authentic expressions of Infinite Mystery—even while recognizing that each may harbor its social pathologies or historical sins. Out of the listening and learning that marks authentic dialogue, participants perceive the formation of a world community dedicated to the betterment of humanity and the earth based on a shared spiritual vision. This search for a common foundation of concern, however, cannot be imposed from outside, or uncritically assessed; it must grow from within the heart of the communion that takes place in the silence intrinsic to persons in dialogue.

IV

> I left [Europe] as a Christian; found myself a
> Hindu; and I return as a Buddhist, without
> having ceased to be a Christian. I contain all
> three.[10]
>
>   ം—ൟ Raimon Panikkar

Crossing the rocky ravines of his native Catalunya, Spain, Raimon Panikkar is a figure who embodies the spirit of multireligious consciousness. Born to a Spanish Catholic mother and a Hindu father, Panikkar's journey into interreligious dialogue has been intellectually profound and personally stunning. As he grappled with his own priestly vows as a Christian, he also opened himself wide to the grandeur of the Hinduism and Buddhism that flowed through his ancestral veins. One of the pioneering scholars of interreligious dialogue, early on he was aware that the question of multiple religions was of the highest order. This realization drew him to an interior self-examination that he later described as not merely a crossing over to other religions, but "a cross." The depth of the interreligious journey compelled him to ponder in his own heart the roots of Christian conservatism and exclusiveness. Breaking out of structural limits and religious boundaries, Panikkar's thought stands out as a free exploration of the human spirit into the future of consciousness.

Never content with concepts that homogenize or universalize lived experience, Panikkar's voluminous writings explore the distinctiveness of his Catholic-Hindu background, finding in its mystical dimensions a way of approaching linkages and commonalities among traditions. In important groundbreaking studies, he challenges the exclusive possession or uniqueness of Christian revelation that historically confines its sacramental dimensions to confessions of faith.[11] Instead, by living within multiple religious universes, Panikkar discovers the point in which Christ, Trinity, Krishna, and the silence of the Buddha are no longer the preserve of a group of believers, but expand out into their cosmic dimensions.

Students in the course on interreligious dialogue find Panikkar's intellectual honesty inspiring, especially when we critically examine two additional areas of thought: how the praxis of interreligious dialogue is lived out in community and how to conceptualize both the unity and difference that interreligious relations promote. Today's interreligious dialogue is widely practiced among leaders and members of different religions for the purpose of better understanding each other and of healing historical misconceptions or sins. Interreligious dialogue also is a powerful force in bringing religious parties together in towns and cities across the globe to jointly tackle issues affecting local communities, including hunger, poverty, rape, homelessness, and gang violence. In addition, a multi-faith orientation is particularly valuable in situations where diversity of belief is common, such as educational settings, hospitals, prisons, and hospice centers.

On a pastoral level, interfaith relations have been going on for centuries, as Panikkar's familial background attests. Marriages between members of different religious traditions—for example, Hindu and Jew or Muslim and Christian, and the raising of their children—occur with increasing regularity today. Specific pastoral issues, including premarital counseling, wedding and baptismal ceremonies, marriage and family guidance, religious observance, and spiritual direction require new skills and education in an interfaith context. These human situations help us to learn about and develop empathy for the many confessions of faith that populate our planet. They also encourage creative expression as clergy and participants learn to develop worship services, liturgies, and prayers for an interreligious world. Another welcome development in pastoral settings is the growing formation of interfaith churches, interfaith spiritual direction programs, intermonastic cooperation, and doctoral programs on interreligious dialogue.

A variety of ideas and models have been advanced to assist in understanding the reality of multiple traditions and prophetic figures. One of the more well-known proposals conceptualizes religious differences as converging in a mystical realm of unity. Here, differences in belief among religions are said to exist only at the historical or phenomenal level. In higher states of mystical consciousness, religious differences are overcome by oneness. The majority of seminary students loosely hold this view when they enter into study. Yet, while helpful in emphasizing harmony over discord, difficulties arise when we try to reconcile conflicting religious claims or ultimate paths. Initial feelings of understanding can quickly dissolve as participants in authentic dialogue probe deeper into the root causes of their beliefs, fears, and faith experiences. Further, as a philosophical attitude, the mystical vision of oneness can become blinded to the real value and spiritual importance of faith differences. By emphasizing a unifying transcendence over embodiment and cultural context, it also can be guilty of suppressing gender, racial, or sexual diversity or denying historical sins rooted in a religion's core precepts. At the same time, mystical oneness is the premier vision that ties the world's religions into an enduring whole. My emphasis in these discussions is, thus, on the complementary and embodied, rather than dualistic and transcendent, relationship between manyness and oneness. The magnificent diversity of religious faiths is, as Abraham Heschel said, "the will of God."[12] Both diversity and oneness reside together in our bodies, minds, and souls. They interpenetrate and indwell in each other in a nondual, inseparable relationship. That is, experiences of unity or oneness evident in mystical events include and celebrate the many manifestations of the world's sacred traditions.

True unity and true communion are never at the expense of difference. Every religion is sustained by a vision of oneness at its core. Every religious tradition brings to the heart of the faithful a unique and stunning vision of ultimate reality. The very existence of these religious lineages is sacred. Mystical unity does not reduce a religion's difference but empowers and fulfills its coming to wholeness in the mind or soul of the individual. When we enter a religion in its depth, when we become one with its wisdom, then we know that it is *both* uniquely true *and* the source that points beyond itself to greater and ever more incomprehensible mysteries. One way I ponder these issues is to envision that the collective fullness of the human spiritual journey is already accessible to our individual consciousness at birth. Because the world's religions tell us that the depth of the person is undefiled in its Source, each of us participates (to varying degrees) in the fullness of reality. Our religious upbringing and education bring into awareness one aspect of this fullness—Hindu, Lakota Sioux, Christian, and so forth—while other religious universes remain latent and not consciously available. As we study, practice, and learn more deeply about the many religious paths, we activate and make conscious these latent religious dimensions, and we embody and cocreate new meanings and ways of knowing reality. Thus, the depth or soul dimension of the person simultaneously is greater than or beyond each religious universe and is structurally receptive to the particular spiritual or religious tradition passed on by one's family and cultural group.

Students learn from these discussions that the capacity to hold in one's soul multiple religious experiences requires a true conversion of heart. It requires, as well, an attitude of receptivity that welcomes God to advance into one's soul and to build in the fibers of one's being a unitive consciousness and an excessive faith greater than our divisions.

V

> *Interreligious dialogue is the distinctive*
> *spiritual journey of our time.*[13]
> ᴓ Ewert Cousins

Interreligious dialogue has broad spiritual implications. Many participants in the interreligious movement agree with

Ewert Cousins that dialogue and interest in other traditions is "the distinctive spiritual journey of our time."[14] In using the language of the spiritual journey, Cousins infers that interreligious and interfaith dialogue is the work of the spirit in us. It involves more than a cognitive and practical component but is a faith journey that activates the soul's latent desire to grow closer to God. Individuals who practice interfaith spirituality do not set out to construct a new religion; they are drawn by an interior call to a living faith experience. In the recesses of their own being, they are stirred to enact an openness to others and to step outside the confines of their own stories. As a journey of faith, interreligious spirituality leads us into the wilderness to experience the change of heart, doubt, fear, happiness, and illumination that grip all genuine spiritual seekers.

This collective spiritual journey is being forged in the present human situation and as such is generating a multitude of questions, some answerable, and others beyond our current ability to know. As a faith commitment, individuals recognize in their hearts that they are living out a sacred vow to practice and to struggle toward communion with all of life. People who heed this spiritual pilgrimage walk with an experience of God as the fountain of peace and nonviolence. Because of its stunning vision of benevolence, interfaith spirituality is a journey without a map, requiring a leaving of the past for the cocreation of an unknown future. This new spiritual path is founded on the oneness and interaction of divine-human-cosmic dimensions.

Interfaith spirituality dwells in the depth of the religious quest, where the Divine spontaneously floods our souls and breaks open our hearts. It is a vision of wholeness on the other side of everything that is partial or fragmented. Interfaith spirituality requires a momentary abandonment of oneself and one's religion in order to find the strength of soul necessary to uphold the vision—exalted in the world's sacred texts—of a unified creation. One does not just read about, study, or think through interfaith spirituality, but *bears* it in one's whole being. If we want to foster a world community based on friendship, humility, and peace, we must embark on an interior journey to heal ourselves of subtle forms of religious possession, violence, and superiority that generate harshness and contempt toward the "other." This inner change of heart becomes the mystical precursor into another, more holistic view of reality.

Interreligious, interfaith dialogue is founded on the contemplative basis of all religions and the need to dwell in the core silence that stabilizes and enriches every religious form. For all the diversity of ideas, religions, and practices found in the world's religions, interreligious dialogue revolves around the Great Silence. In silence, there is no religion to divide or segregate. There is not a Buddhist silence or a Christian silence or a Jewish silence. Only silence. In contemplation, we sink into the silent dimension of reality that is the unifying element in a personal encounter with the religious heritage of human-kind. Silence illuminates all things, bringing into relief our fears, anxieties, harsh words, and unholy thoughts. It releases the source of our passion to know ultimate things, to be holy.

Beneath the sharing of traditions and the participation in each other's sacred rituals and rites, are the mighty waters of *another way*. This way is founded on passive or receptive contemplation, when we are open to the action of Mystery on us. Its process is deconstructive, taking us away from the illusion that we can force, create, or think through a sacred reality beyond the senses. Normal spiritual activities that give comfort or meaning are suspended or inoperable. In these dark encounters with faith, we are flooded with a divine light that we cannot see. We are confronted with a mystical injunction that suspends the claim of any defined religion or spirituality in order to travel the steep and arduous path to the source of a question: Is God, Reality Itself on the side of openness, oneness, manyness, and the community of the spirit? Not susceptible to intellectual agreement or theological imperative, this question demands something more primary: the transformation of the self.

The way of purgative or passive contemplation heals the sin of "otherness"—the exclusion, violence, and rejection of difference—in our hearts. It diminishes spiritual and religious egoism in which one's truth, path, or scripture is secretly or overtly proclaimed to be greater, holier, or truer than any of its competitors. Contemplation, as the force of letting go, also frees us from disguised forms of religious selfishness or pride that harbor a privileged place of salvation, enlightenment, or predestination. Signifying the deep basis of relationship between persons, communities, and spirit, a contemplative attitude is central to the communion that draws the world together.

At the core of the contemplative vision is peace and nonviolence. Based on the experiential realization that the Divine loves the world as one family—animal, plant, mineral, human—interfaith spirituality attends to the well-being of the whole. The practice of nonviolence leads us to understand that interfaith dialogue is first and foremost a quality of soul. It is not the bringing together of disparate religions to find a least common denominator oneness. It is not primarily the discovery of a new religion, although new religious traditions are often born of it. Rather, it is a breaking free of the bondage of exclusiveness that pushes others outside the circle of love.

It is a quality of being that honors, celebrates, and protects the variety and beauty of creation. Both measure and end, a contemplative heart is also the means by which one lives and practices global spirituality.

Chapter SIX

Communion That Surpasses Words

Casa Maria, a Catholic Worker mission, runs a soup kitchen in South Tucson. Each day it serves more than one thousand meals to homeless and indigent people. On a daily basis volunteers from Tucson's varied congregations make a difference in the lives of people pushed to the margins of society. Father Ricardo, a Catholic priest based in the Hispanic community, has been supportive of the Casa Maria community since its beginnings. For almost forty years, he has walked the streets and highways of southern Arizona ministering to the poor. A committed activist and self-professed "extrovert," he also has deep respect, mixed with a tinge of humor, for the more contemplative souls among us.

One of the first people I met when I arrived in Tucson, Ricardo was instrumental in helping me launch the interfaith church and seminary efforts. Wildly committed to all things for peace, our respective engagements with activism and contemplation naturally blend. Yet confronted with the poverty, mental illness, drug addictions, and family upheaval that weigh on the people who come for their daily box lunch, it is difficult at times to see the connection. How does interreligious dialogue help the people at Casa Maria? What is the relationship between contemplation and activism? How can the spiritual dimensions of dialogue contribute to finding solutions to worldwide suffering, combat religiously motivated violence, or alleviate the hunger in a child's belly?

Thomas Merton—the American trappist monk and writer—asked himself similar questions. In his autobiography, *The Seven Storey Mountain*, Merton traces the process that eventually converts him from the trappings and high life of New York City to a cloistered monastery centered on Christ in the hills of Kentucky. This tension between action and contemplation figures predominantly in Merton's writings and is resolved after years of internal debate in his mature recognition that contemplation is at the center of radical social transformation.

Early on Merton moves away from a literary and academic career, working at Friendship House in Harlem under the direction of Catherine de Hueck Doherty. Initially drawn to religious social work, he might have continued in that direction had he not gone on retreat at Gethsemani Abbey. Later, when the question of social activism again pressed on him in the monastery, he sustained an extraordinary correspondence with the prominent theologian Rosemary Radford Reuther, who was critical of the ascetic strain associated with monks. Yet within the walls of the monastic enclosure Merton practiced an unconventional activism that drew from the well of the human spirit. He gave himself to the study of other religions, secular philosophies, and political critiques all within the context of a silence that mends the illusory divide between solitude and service.

I

> *In the night of our technological barbarism,*
> *monks must be as trees which exist silently in*
> *the dark and by their vital presence purify the*
> *air.*[1]
>
> &—∂ Thomas Merton

Since the 1960s, interreligious dialogue has evolved into a new phase characterized by the terms "interspiritual," "intermonastic," or "intercontemplative" dialogue. Wayne Teasdale—scholar and lay interreligious monk—spent many years in India under the tutelage of Father Bede Griffiths, who initiated him into the way of *sannyasa*, a life devoted to renunciation and the quest for God. Teasdale coined the term "interspirituality" to emphasize that a person's ability to assimilate multiple spiritual realities is already present in his or her ontological coding. The prefix "inter" is used to describe the ontological roots that tie the various religious traditions together and mark their interdependence upon each other and their responsibility to humanity and all of creation. Thus, interspirituality is the assimilation of ideas, values, and practices of the world's traditions that enhance the development of one's own spiritual life.[2] I prefer the term "intercontemplative" rather than "interspirituality" or "intermonastic," because it signifies mature interiority and one not confined to the professional monk. Rather, monastic consciousness and the capacity to dwell in silence are common to humanity, allowing us to think of the monk as a universal dimension in all people.

"Intermonastic" dialogue can be traced to the exchange between monastics East and West, especially between Buddhist and Christian monks. In 1960 the world's Benedictine and Cistercian monasteries created the Alliance for International Monasticism (AIM). This secretariat, along with Vatican

II (1962–65), fostered the church's relationship with other religions and urged Christian monks and nuns to pursue mutual understanding with monastics of other faiths. The dialogue of monastics and contemplatives represents one of the most authentic types of interfaith dialogue—the dialogue of religious experience. As monks of different traditions came together, they realized that the most significant focus of monastic interreligious dialogue was the sharing of each others' search for the absolute regardless of their status or religion. These precious treasures of centuries of monastic experience, passed down from person to person and heart to heart, became indispensable to the field.

In 1968 AIM sponsored the first Asian East-West intermonastic conference in Bangkok. It was this conference that brought Thomas Merton to the East and eventually to his visit with His Holiness the Dalai Lama. It was also at this conference that Merton tragically died soon after giving his speech on the second day. Considered by many to be the founding thinker in the West of intermonastic dialogue, Merton was in the vanguard of a new kind of global mysticism that was working itself out in his own soul struggles with monasticism. Ahead of his time, Merton maintained a stubborn refusal to go along with whatever gained the latest currency without first subjecting his intellect and heart to all kinds of testing. He was inoculated against the trendy or smart, and spiritually expedient or contrived, in part because his soul simply was not in it. He knew that his monastic vocation, perhaps seen by others to be a parochial or even elite affair, was the leaven that expanded his solitary search for God into a universal concern for life itself. Merton realized that deep spiritual experience and the contemplative vow to seek union with God were the center point of unity in dialogue with other religions.

Like other contemplative activists of his era, Merton was profoundly committed in the fifties and early sixties to confronting a series of social questions, among them the Cold War, nuclear arms, the peace movement, the civil rights movement, third world oppression, and the materialism of modern America. Merton corresponded with and personally met many similarly minded people, among them Dorothy Day, co-founder of the Catholic worker, and the Jewish mystic and scholar, Abraham Heschel. An admirer of activism, he was deeply touched by their witness to peace and their commitment to nonviolence. The tragedy of the Vietnam War also brought Merton and Buddhist monk and activist Thich Nhat Hanh together. In 1967 Thich Nhat Hanh came on a peace mission to Gethsemani Abbey, and Merton felt an immediate kinship, considering him a spiritual brother. Nhat Hanh's commitment to promote harmony among religions and an international peace movement were issues dear to Merton as well. The next year, on his fateful trip to Asia, Merton spent three days with His Holiness the Dalai Lama, the exiled Tibetan leader, in Dharmasala, India. Merton and the Dalai Lama developed a close friendship, discussing monastic practices, enlightenment, and the role of monks in the world. His Holiness the Dalai Lama "told Merton that he understood the monk as a person 'for the world,' and Merton, in turn, defined the vocation of monks like themselves in public terms, as a calling to be 'living examples of the freedom and transformation of consciousness which meditation can give.'"[3]

Each of these individuals was steeped in his or her respective religious traditions and drew sustenance from centuries of wisdom. These spiritual leaders also were engaged in and committed to the dialogue of religious experience as vital to his or her own spiritual integrity. Like them, Merton recognized that in the deepest demands of contemplative practice, tradition as (denominational or tribal) exclusion gives way to tradition as compassion for and suffering with others. It was not intellectual prowess that sustained this vision, but the capacity within each of their hearts to enter into other worldviews and live them as their own.

Merton threw himself with unabated passion into the spiritual practices and religious experiences of Hindus, Sufis, Jews, Buddhists, and Taoists, among others. From the perspective of spiritual experience, Merton had a deep appreciation and respect for the beauty and wisdom of the world's religions. Studying Zen, Hesychasm, Kabbalah, and a myriad of other practices and traditions, Merton found the point of silence in which he lived and breathed within a sacred universe different than his own, not as a visitor but as a member of the great mystery of being. He absorbed within himself the beauty of diverse religious faiths without abandoning or diminishing the imprint the Eucharist, Trinity, or Sophia exerted on his soul. While Merton chaffed against church precepts and monastic rules, he nonetheless had the utmost respect for Christianity's mystical wisdom and sacramental mysteries. Nothing that was imbued with spirit, nothing that evoked the Divine, was segregated from his consciousness. Merton felt it was his duty to find in himself the unifying vision at the heart of Christian monasticism that could lead to mutual religious respect and reconciliation. His quest to serve as a bridge between East and West, and between Christian contemplation and secular materialism, was founded on his conviction that only in and through dialogue with the world around him could he find his true self.

Wide open to the spirit, Merton pursued monastic conversation wherever and with whomever he could. He understood that monasticism was not the special preserve of vowed monks but the archetype of solitude present in the deep self. By whichever name—intermonastic, interspiritual, or intercontemplative—dialogue is based on the mature exchange of religious experiences. Rooted in the techniques of spiritual enlightenment (prayer, meditation, and self-emptiness), participants find that by sharing practical experiences and learning from each other's mystical traditions, they uncover a new spiritual path for humanity. The dialogue of contemplatives draws not only on the primary roots that nourish and bind together our religious heritages, but also supports the growth of new branches on the mother tree of human spirituality.

II

> *To love spiritually is to feel compassion, and*
> *whoever feels compassionate loves most.*[4]
> ◠◡◠ Miguel de Unamuno

The ecumenical encounter for Merton began with his mystical experience on the streets of Louisville, Kentucky, and led to his conviction that there is an essential unity of all human beings realized in contemplative experience and founded in the common ground of love. Dispelled of the illusion that his monastic vows made him a special being, Merton later wrote, "I was suddenly overwhelmed with the realization that I loved all those people, that they were mine and I theirs."[5] While his immediate apprehension of oneness is the quintessential mystical insight, Merton understood that his vision was also deeply personal and interior. He realized that the unity of humanity and the healing of divisions first must take place in mending his own soul.

> Ancient and traditional societies, whether of Asia or
> of the West, always specifically recognized "the way"
> of the wise . . . in which some [persons] would attain
> to the inner meaning of being, they would *experience*
> this meaning for all their brothers [and sisters], they
> would so to speak bring together in themselves the
> divisions or complications that confused the life of
> their fellows. By healing the divisions in themselves
> they would help heal the divisions of the whole
> world.[6]

In a parable titled "The Fasting of the Heart," based on a translation from Chuang Tzu, Merton clarified his contemplative approach to social change that seeks for a real change of heart. To find true unity, to be free from limitation and preoccupation with self-awareness, he suggests a fast of the heart. In Merton's parable, Yen Hui, a disciple of Confucius, decides to enter politics and save the state from a corrupt king. Asked by Confucius how he will subdue the king and bring about justice, Yen Hui explains that he will outwardly appear to yield while remaining disinterested and uncompromising inside. By tempering his ambition and even his belief that he is superior in nonviolence, Yen Hui practices the fast of the heart. Chuang Tzu explains that the goal of fasting is an inner unity and freedom in which we hear with our whole being, with our spirits and hearts, and not just with the ear.

A similar vision was held by Howard Thurman, African-American mystic and theologian. The impetus for his radical commitment to nonviolence and mystical social change was premised on his testimony that life moves in the direction of unity. Against the fragmentation of racism that shatters lives and divides people against themselves, Thurman labored to join others into a single harmony. Through his many peace initiatives—including his founding of an interreligious and culturally plural church—Thurman, like Merton, "realized that what troubles modern individuals is the moral insignificance of their lives. . . .[Each] was a spokesman for the soul, the deep self, the sublime—a 'sign of refusal' to the ways of the world."[7]

III

> *When the mendicant monks (*bhikku*) come together, they should do one of two things: either talk about the Dharma or maintain a noble silence.*[8]
>
> ⌒⊙ Majihima-nikaya

Silence and solitude underlie the spiritual practice of all contemplatives and the rhythm of the monastic day: prayer, meditation, study, writing, work, and community. Of these, the greatest is silence. The contemplative life Merton advocated taught that by penetrating our own silence we discover what is beyond words and explanations and thereby experience the intimate union of God in the secret point of our soul. Central to all meditative traditions, silence is the catalyst that draws us to feel the web of communion that sustains life. Merton felt that the monk had a special task to realize within himself or herself a universal consciousness. Through sadness and joy, aloneness and despair, the solitary person purifies the heart and prepares a dwelling within oneself to pour out the sorrow and love of the world.

Merton possessed a global spiritual consciousness premised on a distinctive mystical vision of the person. In the deep caverns of the inner self, God and the soul are always alone, yet always universal; "for in this inmost 'I' my own solitude meets the solitude of every other man [and woman] and the solitude of God."⁹ By joining the wisdom of the East with that of the West, Merton believed intermonastic exchanges would be deepened, allowing entrance into each other's world of meaning and spiritual source. During his travels to Asia, Merton wrote further about the dynamics of sharing spiritual truths with persons of a different faith. Dividing contemplative dialogue into three levels—the preverbal, verbal, and the postverbal—he developed an "intertraditional vocabulary" that encouraged intelligent discussion of all kinds of religious experience across traditions.[10]

> The "preverbal" level is that of the unspoken and indefinable "preparation," the "predisposition" of mind and heart, necessary for all "monastic" experience whatever . . . [The monk] must be wide open to life and to new experience because he has fully utilized his own tradition and gone beyond it. This will permit him to meet a disciple of another apparently remote and alien tradition and find a common ground of verbal understanding with him. The "postverbal" level will . . . be that on which both meet beyond their own words and their own understanding in the silence of an ultimate experience which might conceivably not have occurred if they had not met and spoken. . . . This I would call 'communion.' I think it is something that the deepest ground of our being cries out for, and it is something for which a lifetime of striving would not be enough."[11]

The postverbal level fosters an atmosphere conducive to silence and solitude. In this way, we sink into a depth of being that echoes the rhythm of the monastic day, allowing the rhythm of silence to become the matrix for dialogue itself. Silence itself is the teaching. Words fall away and draw us inward beyond our differences and confusions to the same silence, because being one, silence unites. Abraham Heschel called this practice of silence "depth theology" to indicate that real theology is a spiritual event that takes place in the heart. When we discover inner silence, there are no divisions but only communion and intimacy. Heschel's "depth theology" is really the experience of the dark light of contemplation where no names are given and God confronts us not through names or through the medium of nature but in the desert of divine simplicity.

IV

> *Monks beg for food in humble robes, their daily*
> *actions being one with the Way.*[12]
>
>   Dogen

Central to the mature contemplative vocation is the practice of humility, by which the heart is honed and tested and the artifacts of personality are fired in detachment and let go. Followers of the monastic way are called to purity of heart, for a humble heart is the great equalizer and the bitter medicine necessary to draw out the sweetness of being. For the vow of the monk—and by extension the unspoken oath of every sentient being—is to be for others, to be universal, and not for the self alone. Applied to religious dialogue, and to the suffering of creation, Heschel held "humility and contrition" to be necessary conditions of a pure heart. He called for a healing of religious differences based on his understanding of the biblical command to mercy and humility. Heschel believed that humility is the secret test of faith. Since every religion claims to be true, certitude belies the fact that truth is not fully accessible to the mind. Only humility can show us the proper path, only humility is prior to certitude and more foundational than claim. Heschel held that religious diversity is the will of God at this time in history. Because religious pluralism is part of God's design, he upheld its necessity with prophetic conviction. God wants us to cooperate and be at peace; it is God's will that we reach out to each other's religions to embrace the one divine presence in many forms. Humility is the guiding means, the fear and trembling, that brings us to the practice of spiritual dialogue.

Mahatma Gandhi also prayed for and practiced the "manyness" of truth as an essential commandment. Humility and nonviolence were intimately connected to religious openness, for true dialogue is the fruit of an unceasing commitment to nonharm or *ahimsa*. Applied to communion among spiritual practitioners, Gandhi practiced *ahimsa* as the guiding means that checks our natural tendencies to judge or punish. Reflecting the highest virtue of humility, nonharm affirms the divine injunction to respect the dignity of every religion and life form. Merton echoes a similar commitment. He understood humility to be the bitter fruit of a kind of rejection from the world that all women and men of true purpose suffer. Because they are outside their own times, they are wounded by their uniqueness and wisdom into a final perfection and a silence in which they speak for all people, known and unknown, who can understand the simplicity of the spirit.

A practical and enlightened outgrowth of spiritual humility is exemplified in the monastic principles that inform Monastic Interreligious Dialogue. Created in 1978 as the North American subcommittee of AIM, Monastic Interreligious Dialogue

(MID) encourages monasteries of the Benedictine tradition to enter into contact with monastics of other religions. Its three guiding principles recall the innovation of St. Benedict and the centuries of contemplative wisdom archived in the world's religions. Reflecting the spirit of monastic hospitality, contemplation, and ethical involvement, I quote excerpts from these principles below.

> *Hospitality.* The first concerns hospitality. Interreligious dialogue expands the ancient practice of monastic hospitality. It is no longer just a matter of welcoming guests to the monastery, sharing our prayer and table with them, conversing with them. Hospitality involves welcoming the spirituality of the other as a valid path to God, seeing in its charism and practices an expression of a monastic intuition common to all humanity. . . .

> *Contemplation.* The second concerns contemplation. Spiritual exchanges and interreligious prayer with contemplatives of other religions provide Christian monastics with the possibility of becoming familiar with and adopting certain of their methods of prayer and meditation (for example, Vipassana, Zazen, Yoga). Intermonastic dialogue can be a way of enriching our understanding and appreciation of contemplation, and also of recovering parts of our own tradition, for example, attention to the details of daily life, openness to the cosmos, the importance of the body.

> *Ethical Involvement.* The third concerns ethical, social, and political involvement: Spiritual exchanges

strengthen the bonds between believers of different
religious traditions and promote their collaboration in
the initiatives that religions have undertaken to bring
about peace and to protect the environment.[13]

Founded on a mystical orientation, intermonastic dialogue directs us to discover the interior unity that heals divisions between self and others, and God and creation. It also
employs the spiritual practices of our traditions—prayer, meditation, silence, and solitude—as a foundation for a life committed to openness and generosity. In the dialogue of religious
experience, participants direct the virtues of humility, mercy,
compassion, selfless love, and nonviolence toward reverence
for human and nonhuman life. These deep spiritual principles are necessary to alleviate suffering and oppression and
to transform social, political, religious, and economic institutions. The prophets, mystics, saints, and monks of our time
have embarked on the stormy seas of an intercontemplative
journey in search of the promised shores of global peace.

V

Humble sentient beings, completely suppressed
by seemingly endless and terribly intense,
negative deeds, May all their fears from
unbearable war, famine, and disease be pacified,
to quickly stem the flow of blood and tears.[14]
    ❧ Dalai Lama

Both advocates and critics of interreligious dialogue insist
that it has been less than effective in addressing concrete historical conditions, and that it must enter a new phase of engaged
contact with the world. In order to understand the suffering

and ameliorate the oppression of the perceived "other," to combat the religiously motivated violence that has marred religious history, and to work together toward a global community of right human and planetary relations, intellectual dialogue or even shared religious concern is not enough.

At the 1993 Parliament of the World's Religions, Paul Knitter, professor of theology at Xavier University, raised an important concern that in affirming pluralism we do not become segregated from crushing issues of violence and subjugation that afflict our world today. The question Knitter posed—what is the value of interreligious relations if they remain in the personal, cognitive, or even group dimension without concurrent socioecological liberation?—is crucial to the future of our planet. Taking this question into the social arena, Knitter suggests "that the balance between pluralism and oppression is not an equal balancing. The reality of oppression must have a *priority in the contents* of our interfaith dialogue, and the voices of the oppressed peoples and oppressed earth must have a *'hermeneutical privilege' in our dialogical deliberations.*"[15] Given the inequalities in our world today and the way those inequalities are created and sustained by economic, political, and military powers, dialogue must become committed to creating an environment in which those who historically are left out of the conversation feel welcomed and unthreatened to speak at the table of discourse.

The universality of suffering on our planet ruptures our categories and interpretations, sensitizing us to the responsibility religions have to create a global environment in which the voices of underrepresented or ignored peoples and groups are brought to the discussion table. Similarly, feminist scholars argue that the interreligious focus on *religious* differences has effectively ignored the spiritual oppression of women and their struggles with racism, sexism, or poverty. In addition, it has not led to the inclusion of multiple interpretations of meaning derived specifically from women's experiences and concerns. Knitter holds: "Between nations, and within nations, there are power structures and socioeconomic disparities that do not allow all to have equal voice. And so, when we approach 'the others' in dialogue, it is not sufficient to affirm and open ourselves to their *difference*, . . . we must also affirm their freedom and dignity. And if such *freedom and dignity* are lacking, then we must act to make them possible. To delight in difference, but to be unconcerned about dignity, is to be only half-human in reaching out to the other."[16]

Knitter raises critical issues. The most successful campaigns to affirm dignity have arisen through the application of nonviolent principles to eliminate concrete instances of injustice and oppression. A contemplative focus alerts us to how violation of spiritual integrity and equality wounds our bodies but also our souls. Nonviolence insists that dialogue must take into account and bring to the world's attention the great sorrow that is generated from collective destruction and abuse of the sacred in our world. Social witness is intrinsic to interfaith spirituality because it is the process by which the goal of the mystical life—oneness with all life—can be actualized in our institutions, nations, and relations. Only when we recognize the voices of those who are absent from dialogue because of systematic hunger or social and political oppression will we find the way to truly have a global conversation.

Although overlooked in most cultural indicators, contemplative consciousness has been a driving force behind some of the twentieth century's most important political and social achievements. From his monastic hermitage, Merton spoke *against* the Cold War, Vietnam, and materialism, and spoke *for* nonviolence, peace, and love. Similarly, Heschel not only felt it was his sacred duty to restore the soul of the Jewish people suffering from the atrocities of the Nazi Holocaust, but also to stand in solidarity with oppression wherever it is found. Marching alongside Martin Luther King, Jr., this contemporary prophet resonated with everything life-giving and flourishing in the human spirit. Like Merton and Heschel, Thurman was not only spiritually ahead of his time, he was also a champion of religious diversity, intercultural and interreligious communication, and a tireless advocate for the spiritual integrity that sustained the Civil Rights Movement. Each of these men drew inspiration not only from their respective religions but also from the phenomenal spiritual experiment unfolding across the great continent of India. In Mahatma Gandhi, each found a kindred soul that fostered their own commitment to nonviolent social activism.

Events in Asia triggered the modern world's first spiritually motivated political campaign in Mohandas K. Gandhi's movement for nonviolence that spanned the first fifty years of the twentieth century. Drawing on centuries of Hindu, Jain, and Buddhist wisdom, Gandhi forged a stunning exemplar of contemplative activism. From his ashrams and communities, he ran a pervasive political campaign that was instrumental in routing the British from Indian soil. Using what he considered to be the greatest weapon of all—the moral superiority of nonviolence—Gandhi's fierce spiritual commitment branded into global awareness the potency of contemplation engaged in the service of social change. Behind every tactic and victory in the Mahatma's arsenal lay the spiritual imperatives of silence, fasting, prayer, and sacrifice. Intertwined with Indian independence, was a monastic commitment to refuse the trappings of social comfort or political expediency for the sake of suffering souls everywhere. Honest in his admission that his efforts were not purely selfless, Gandhi wrote that what he was striving to achieve in his political campaigns was self-realization, to see God face-to-face.

Prayer was the center of Gandhi's life. "Without it, he wrote, "I should have been a lunatic long ago."[17] Rooted in the ancient and beloved Hindu scripture, the *Bhagavad Gita*, which he recited every day, Gandhi included Christian, Islamic, Jain, Sikh, and Buddhist prayers into his morning and evening services. As a devotee of nonviolence, he found companionship in Jesus' sermons, especially the Sermon on the Mount from the Gospel of Matthew. Gandhi's all-consuming passion to alleviate suffering was inextricably linked to his faith in the nonviolence of God. Prayer was his time of communion with the God of peace. It was a daily practice that strengthened his resolve to find in nonviolence the political equivalent of the *sannyasin's* quest for purity of heart.

Profoundly influenced by writings on nonviolence and civil disobedience, Gandhi synthesized in his life the world's scriptures and the thought of other pioneers of peace, including the works of Henry David Thoreau and Leo Tolstoy. His legacy of ultimate commitment to self-sacrifice and *ahimsa* in the name of sufferers everywhere inspired vows of poverty and nonviolence in Merton, Thurman, Day, King, and numerous other souls. During the Montgomery boycott, for example, King later wrote: "Nonviolent resistance had emerged as the technique of the movement, while love stood as the regulating ideal. In other words, Christ furnished the spirit and motivation, while Gandhi furnished the method."[18]

The vows of nonviolence and personal sacrifice developed by Tolstoy, Gandhi, and King listed below serve to illustrate the interdependence of spiritual principles, positive social change, and faith-based nonviolence in transforming attitudes and systems that contribute to global suffering.

Leo Tolstoy's Five Commandments Based on the Sermon on the Mount[19]

- Have no ill-will against anyone, but love all.
- Be completely chaste, even in thought.
- Live only in the present and do not worry about the future.
- Never use violence or repay evil with evil but suffer insult and give up possessions.
- Love our enemies and those who hate us by treating them as ourselves.

Vows Taken by Members of Gandhi's Satyagraha Ashram[20]

- Have a living faith in God.
- Believe in truth and nonviolence as his creed and, therefore, have faith in the inherent goodness of human nature, which he expects to evoke by his truth and love expressed through his suffering.
- Lead a chaste life and be ready and willing for the sake of his cause to give up life and possessions.
- Be free from all intoxicants.
- Pray ceaselessly.
- Be a habitual weaver and spinner of *khadi* (hand-woven cloth).
- Carry out with a willing heart all the rules of discipline as may be laid down from time to time.
- Include multireligious prayers and practices in daily services.

Pledge to Nonviolence Taken by Marchers with Dr. King, 1963[21]

- □ Meditate daily on the life and teachings of Jesus.
- □ Remember that the nonviolent movement seeks justice and reconciliation—not victory.
- □ Walk and talk in the manner of love; for God is love.
- □ Pray daily to be used by God in order that all men and women might be free.
- □ Sacrifice personal wishes that all might be free.
- □ Observe with friend and foes the ordinary rules of courtesy.
- □ Perform regular service for others and for the world.
- □ Refrain from violence of fist, tongue, and heart.
- □ Strive to be in good spiritual and bodily health.
- □ Follow the directions of the movement leaders and of the captains on demonstrations.

VI

*With reverent hymns of peace we should now
sing the praises of God's peace, for it is this
which brings all things together.*[22]
         ✧ Pseudo-Dionysius

Today we are challenged more than ever before to work together toward building Martin Luther King's "beloved community." Through mutual cooperation and sharing we find the means to mend the rifts between rich and poor, spirit and body, hatred and compassion. In attaining inner peace, we discover new answers to perpetual human problems—poverty, racism, ecological degradation, violence against women, war, starvation, and moral temerity. Through the witness and lives of modern saints, we learn to direct mystical consciousness in the service of societal reform. For these women and men, devotion to nonviolence is the secret force in political liberation and in freedom from all forms of oppression: physical, economic, religious, spiritual, and soul. Inner peace can never be achieved at the expense of historically marginalized groups of people. True concern for humanity and the earth challenges us to probe our inner lives and to uncover points of spiritual exclusion, violence, superiority, or rejection that wound our souls and diminish love. When we have the courage to face ourselves, we will realize that the real spiritual task begins in searching our own hearts for the inner ground of unity.

Thomas Merton, His Holiness the Dalai Lama, Thich Nhat Hanh, Abraham Heschel, Martin Luther King Jr., and others have devoted themselves to the unification of our differences. In the depth of their own faith, they offered their lives in service to refugees, to those who suffer from racial injustice, to soldiers in war, starving families, survivors of genocide, and other members of the human family whose dignity is debased by calculated violence or indifference. They touched a living stream of life, living an ethical code that was outside traditional ethics, if by ethics we mean the domination of moral strictures developed and enforced by one group. They practiced a circle of compassion that included everyone and excluded no one or no thing, all the while retaining the compunction, humility, tenderness, insight, and sacrifice that hollows out one's soul and prepares it as a vessel of the Divine. In their own suffering and in their own struggle to come to terms with the anguish and violence of their day, they forged a path across the solitary desert sands to the mountaintop of dreams, of the dream of what is to come. They could see it, and the seeing commanded a practicing of what they saw. There was nothing left for them to do but to embody the coming unity, the unity of all the differences in oneself. As Thomas Merton prophetically wrote:

> The deepest level of communication is not communication but communion. It is wordless. It is beyond words, and it is beyond speech, and it is beyond concept. Not that we discover a new unity. My dear brothers [and sisters] we are already one. But we imagine that we are not. And what we have to recover is our original unity.[23]

Chapter SEVEN

Emerging Heart

One of the more moving experiences in my life occurred at the Metropolitan Baptist Church in Harlem. At the time, I was attending a conference on world spirituality with several hundred other representatives from the world's religions. On this day, the whole group of us had been invited to a gospel service. As we filed into the church, Hindu *sannyasins* were seated next to Thai Buddhist monks; the Orthodox prelate shared a pew with the rabbi from Russia. All around me were people of different traditions, races, cultural backgrounds, and religions. As the pastor rose, the gospel choir broke into song and invited the entire congregation to clap, sway, and praise. I joined with Zen monks in somber gray robes, Zoroastrian priests clothed in white cotton, Hopi elders in native dress, and Jain mystics with insect filters covering their mouths to offer our prays in one voice. I cannot claim that the church service was revelatory itself, but the experience certainly was.

It showed me how tangible and real is peace; how the mutual and respectful sharing among peoples and traditions allowed my heart to spring into joy; how this momentary period of respite from an often viciously troubled world brought me to tears for the simple grace of being alive.

This event, one too seldom experienced in our world today, is part of my hidden longing. The experience was symbolic of how community rises out of contemplation and how great shifts in human planetary history begin with the actions of a small group of individuals longing to live another way. I felt in people a desire to love differently, to practice what their hearts felt, as if what they felt was too large for the kind of love they were told was enough. In the presence of our swaying, rocking congregation, I found an expansion of our souls. As we pressed up against old biases and ancient enmities palpable in the air, instead of suffocating under the weight of so much history a collective heart was born. Out of an unknown depth, we became cocreators of an emerging global consciousness and a new dream for our earth.

I

> *This new language of prayer has to come out of something which transcends all our traditions, and comes out of the immediacy of love.*[1]
> — Thomas Merton

What I learned that day and through all the other days over these last thirty years is that our common spirituality—our global spirituality—is forged together by the prayer of love that transcends religions. It is not a reality that is conceived and constructed by the mind, but a state of consciousness we discover is already present by surrendering ourselves to or sinking down into the spiritual core of life. Global spirituality is an affair of the heart that begins deep within one's soul and is the soul's active expression of the unity of creation that sustains diversity and difference rather than marginalizing those differences. Global spirituality is not solely concerned with the coming together of different religions, but with following a divine call to love in a new way, *to be holier.* It is a sacred experience on the human horizon that is drawing people toward a mystical, rather than religious expression of faith. For in the mystical traditions, the heart is not primarily the seat of emotions and feelings, but the place that draws us inward and helps us to dwell in our spiritual center.

Not confined to religions, global spirituality is predicated on the faith that a new breaking in of the Divine is available for all of the human community today. While we cannot fully comprehend its vastness or nature, we are granted a precious opportunity to offer our own beings as the birth place of a new spiritual life. This breaking in of divinity frees us from elements in our collective religious heritage that are oppressive, socially unconscious, or institutionally self-absorbed. We are challenged to rethink our religious stories, reevaluate our notions of God, cocreate new practices and traditions; and discover new dimensions of reality unknown or unexplored. Global spirituality dwells in the silent spaces that take us back to the beginning, to the structures of consciousness that have given rise to diverse religious worldviews over these many centuries. It provides new practices and ways of being and knowing that lead to the creation of spiritual traditions for our time.

Global spirituality seeks to actualize the promise of all the religions of the world—that we can achieve spiritual harmony on earth. It recognizes that this task cannot be accomplished through a collective consciousness that still perceives God, the

Real, as separate from the person or creation, or as a punishing, vengeful force. A global spiritual perspective requires a shift in orientation to a God of peace and nonviolence; and from a distant, unfeeling divinity to an experience of the Divine as intimacy itself, immeasurably close to our hearts. It emphasizes that the Divine is the source of benevolence and unification, and is the force of liberation of the heart. It also opens up the individualized and communal consciousness of axial and tribal religions to a multidimensional consciousness. This multi-dimensional awareness probes the wholeness of things through an interpretive stance that takes into account personal and social (including political, cultural, gender, and racial) differences, the fate of the earth, and the sacred realities that impact on our spirits and on the flourishing of life on earth.

On a practical level, global spirituality asks us to consider: How can the spiritual disciplines I practice, and the value I derive from my personal relationship with the Divine be of assistance in mitigating the suffering and ills of the world? How can the wisdom of other traditions enrich my own religion's beliefs and practices and assist me in overcoming elements that are harmful or oppressive to others? On a personal level, a global spiritual perspective calls us to a greater compassion and to practice the spiritual virtues of love of one's neighbors, altruism, and devotion extolled in the world's scriptures. It is a lived spiritual practice that confronts the assumptions of individualism and self-motivation that permeate our culture today.

Just as the individual spiritual journey is premised on the self's relationship with its divine source, global spirituality is an orientation of compassion that self-consciously directs our actions beyond individualistic motives. It guides us to solidarity with the plural worlds that inhabit our planet—animal, insect, plant, human—and reveals the mysterious bond each shares with its sacred source. Further, global spirituality directs society to the consideration of spiritual values that will lead the world to greater justice and peace. Gandhi's notion of *satyagraha* (soul-force) and *ahimsa* (nonviolence) and Martin Luther King's expression of excessive altruism are two examples of the strength of spiritual principles in making our world a more humane place.

Global spirituality works to sustain a sacred community on earth by bringing the voice of the spirit to matters of common economic, political, ethical, and religious concerns. As engaged practice, global spirituality is an orientation toward life that is concerned about the sacredness of, and reverence for, all human and nonhuman life; deeply committed to how social, political, religious, and economic institutions can be in service of the divinity of the world; and founded on the locus of the spirit, where there is absent a sense of "I" and "mine."

II

> *A vein of sapphires hides in the earth, a*
> *sweetness in fruit. Like these, the Infinite rests*
> *concealed in the heart.*[2]
> ೭_೭ Mahadeviyakka

Through the soul struggles, tears, breakthroughs, and illuminations of the people I have been honored to serve, I know that this new spiritual path is first and foremost a sacred journey. It is the longing in our souls to experience divine union—to see God face-to-face—not only for oneself but for the whole world. It is the dream in our hearts to make possible the divine presence on earth.

Perhaps what is most confounding for people who live this path is that it is almost impossible to describe or name.

There is something in the experience that eludes expression. In part this quandary is due to the fact that many aspects of the journey dismantle old ways of being religious or of being devoted to a spiritual path. It is not that a global or interfaith spirituality has no content or context, it is just that it disrupts every model, role, or identity we use as a crutch. My old friend Meister Eckhart, one of Christianity's most provocative mystics, describes for us his own experience of letting go of all spiritual forms. He tells of three ways to God. The first way is one in which we seek "God in all creatures with manifold activity and ardent longing. . . . The second way is a wayless way, free and yet bound, . . . past self and all things, without will and without images; the third way is called a way, but is really being at home, that is: seeing God without means."[3]

While global spirituality basks in silence and unnaming, there is nothing of meaning or wisdom absent. Every spiritual process, mystical vision, devotional prayer, or sacramental ritual in our collective religious heritage is present but in a different way. It is a form of consciousness that I believe every founder of religion discovered and that those in the vanguard of spirituality live and express. We are taken to the structures and archetypes that inform the master teachings of our world's mystical traditions. Here we experience the reality of cocreation, the dynamic within which the immanence of matter and the consciousness of transcendence unite to give birth to new traditions and spiritual paths in the crucible of dialogue. In the subterranean caverns of the soul, we touch the beginning, point of nothingness, or spark from which the spirit gives rise to forms. No one can say how this happens. Yet we know from recorded accounts and our own experiences that contemplation opens up and unleashes the building blocks of the human spirit.

In contemplation, our bodies, minds, and spirits dwell in the formless form, the placeless place. This is the realm of the beginning, the womb. Here we are in touch with the archetypes of all spiritual worlds already in existence and those coming into form. We find what Zen practitioners call the "face before we were born." Deep states of contemplation put us in touch with the fundamental traditions, the master structures or master narratives that inform every form of consciousness. These master patterns are encoded in our spiritual bodies like DNA is encoded in our genes. In this depth, religious differences do not disappear or become obsolete any more than in the study of DNA genetic differences are erased. In a similar way, contemplation does not refute or eliminate religious and metaphysical distinctions but sees them from the vantage point of their common source or structure, what mystics call "oneness" or "unity." In this mystical depth, the individual is universal or global. What is most important, most prevalent, most real is the unifying force.

III

> *It was I who planted this tree, so that all the world could delight in it, and I engraved all within it, and called its name "the All."*[4]
>
> —Sefer ha-Bahir

Yet the feeling of being thrown off course persists. Friends like Charlie or students in retreats who are living this spiritual life tell me they still have trouble with questions that family members or friends from other religions ask them. There is something fundamental, perhaps even primal, about declaring a new spiritual way, something that touches a deep vein in a person's soul. Questions arise: Does global spirituality have a theology? That is, does it have a comprehensive or systematic foundation for reflecting on ultimate things or God issues? What kind of spiritual practices does one perform?

All I am able to offer comes in fragments and patches from the spiritual lives that I have seen pass before me in spiritual direction. I have learned from these many spiritual friends that they must travel the path of every religion—to leave the false self, to empty oneself out, to become "nothing." They, like you, have moments of illumination and times when the pain of their own partiality, inadequacy, or fear overcomes them. Many have had religious experiences of divine love or compassion; they long to be holier, to draw closer to the divine heart. They recognize, too, that only by giving themselves away will they be capable of living for/in God. Thus, they devote themselves to prayer and meditation; perhaps it is a Buddhist practice they follow; perhaps Jewish. But they know the form is not the most important thing. Most important is their passion to know truth, the longing in their hearts to be reunited with their source.

It is as if through the suffering of having no formalized religion, the Spirit is drawing us to the other side—to the side where love is all encompassing and there is no longer fear of God. It is through this spiritual struggle that we come to understand the path of global spirituality and the unending gift of life. It is here that we begin to grasp our individual part in the restoration of our own souls. This is where the spirit moves inward to greet its mystical beginnings and understands the impact of the unitive spiritual life.

I often am reminded that every spiritual path advances according to the two most important aspects of the inner journey: love of truth alone and emptiness of self. When we put our whole self and our whole passion on love of the Divine, we belong then to the sphere of the holy. It does not matter if we know where we are going or are lost or even have a god with a name. What matters is that we finally give ourselves over to the spirit. By concentrating our whole self on love and longing for God, we forge a path toward the open days of awe. In this way we learn from the interior of our souls; we are taught through the hidden ground of love about spiritual things and the true nature of reality. To love in this way requires the absence of self-interest; it requires a giving away of the false self in order to melt into emptiness or nothingness.

Meister Eckhart knew this mystic path of nothingness so well. He knew that authentic spirituality strips us of self-identity and turns us away from every method or mode. Eckhart also grasped the primary paradox—by giving up identified paths for the wayless way, we simultaneously possess all methods and all ways. Our prayer is "make me empty," "show me how to be nothing" so that I, too, may dwell in your abundance.

IV

> When we enter into the precinct of the hidden
> and invisible, it is sufficient if Truth merely
> whets our knowledge with some meager and
> obscure ideas; and these spiritual drops flow
> through the saints and God's representatives.[5]
> ౨─௶ Gregory of Nyssa

The fruition of global spiritual consciousness situates ourselves in the cave of the heart. Central to monastic spirituality, the image of the cave or hermitage functions to inspire a commitment to seek reality directly. The first and great gift of monasticism is permission to put the eternal human longing for God at the center of one's life. It is a declaration made within one's community, but also to all the world, that we are inspired by and no longer ashamed to admit that longing for enlightenment or union is at the center of our lives. The vows and virtues, commandments and precepts, and solitude and silence associated with monasticism are for the sake of this ideal. The whole journey is propelled by a fervent realization that in silence, *samsara* is *nirvana, atman* is *Brahman,* God and self are one. To be alone is to be simultaneously whole and happy, connected to the source of creation and to all of life. United in this interdependent web of relations, the monk is not for herself or himself but for the whole. In prayer, the individual sinks into that point of unity for the sake of the whole world.

As modern, uncloistered and unvowed, monks we enter a luminous fire. This intensity of being takes apart social conditioning and attachment to material and emotional accumulation in order to uncover or rediscover the one thing necessary: to live for God. The monastic community is never for promotion of social agendas or coercion to a programmed view. To have the monastic spirit is to take a stand as a dissident from social roles in order to find what is more authentic, more real, more truly "right" or in balance with our lives.

Among the many ideals upheld by monastics around the globe is an emphasis on poverty and humility, reverence and prayer, simplicity and gratitude, adoration and rest, obedience and integrity, and freedom of conscience. The monastic heart is not confined to the professional monk, but is a quality of being in all people. While some religious traditions, such as Judaism, do not have a contemporary monastic form, and others like Sufism form lineages or brotherhoods, each of us contains a well of silence that connects to our source. This inner solitute allows us to stand away from or in protest to the merely apparent or the crowd.

As a global community it is helpful to reimagine our world as a spiritual monastery, in which the sacredness of the earth and our life within it are considered in their holiness. Like the professional monk, we are called to uphold an impossible ideal—the coming into our lives of paradise, of the hoped for communion and unity of hearts. This ability to see each other as brother and sister, and to practice compassion, peace, mercy, and forgiveness, provides nourishment for body and soul. We need to cultivate the monastic ideal of living for *Spirit*, rather than for *human ends*, transposing this monastic worldlessness from the individual or group to the well-being of the whole earthly community.

V

> But I say to you who are simple, to give you
> comfort and strength . . . we are all one in love. [6]
> ⟫—◈ Julian of Norwich

As we have seen, mystics the world over emphasize that their most profound insight into reality can be described as "oneness" or "interdependence." Through the veils of creation's great variety and abundance, they discover simplicity, unity, and wholeness. The mystics also teach us that we are compelled to live an ethical imperative, in which oneness and interdependence with all reality becomes the ground of our concern for social justice. The very depth of our love for life, and our gripping awareness of human suffering, requires that we cannot be indifferent to the injustices in our world. Thus, the first and enduring theme in this unfolding age is the personal and social dimension of the *unity of existence*—what the fourteenth-century mystic Julian of Norwich called *one-ing*, or the wandering ascetics of India termed *advaita*—nondualism, "not-two." Evidence of the power of viewing all of creation as interdependent and mutually indwelling is evident in so many of our world religions. Although the unitive voice within our traditions remind us that distance from God is illusion, much of Western spirituality is premised on return from a state of ignorance or sin. I am not implying that the archetype of exile and return simply can be discarded or is without merit. No doubt each of us experiences and suffers alienation, aloneness, and fear of abandonment by God.

What I do contend, however, is that global spiritual consciousness does not emphasize the ancient drama of exodus, wandering, and return. Instead, constituted by unification and integration, it disrupts the story of our beginnings. It begins from a different—but ancient mystical—ontological premise: we are never separated or exiled from the wholeness of our Source. The unity of existence binds our bodies and spirits to the entire cosmos. Our inner journey is not first and foremost ascetic or self-deprecating; in the first instance it is joy, spontaneous eruption of bliss, what we call holiness or sanctification. This is the spark of every being and every consciousness: a spontaneous, intentional joy of being. It is the ultimate, divinity, working itself out in matter. God, or whatever name we assign to Mystery, is fully present in the world. As so many holy teachers have insisted: the Divine dwells in the unity of creation; there is no place empty of the Divine. And because this is so, whenever we give ourselves over to the power of unification and integration, the old confusions, anguishes, and laments are healed or washed away.

Throughout history, spiritual teachers have been in the vanguard of this unitive paradigm. They have lived and taught what the dominant mode of consciousness ignored and suppressed. But despite these numerous teachings of wisdom, the vision of the unity of existence has not become the dominant mode of human consciousness over these many centuries. We are challenged by this emerging age to forge a new understanding of everyday life based on the indwelling presence of Mystery in our bodies, relationships, and political and social institutions. World events, ecological degradation, and human sorrow compel us to embrace and practice the unification of the world, welcoming all creation into the circle of holiness.

If separation and exile structure the ontological wound of human communities in relationship to their divine source, transcendence and distance reflect our religious response to holiness and awe. Global spirituality, however, emphasizes the Divine as immeasurably close, indwelling in our wholeness. Rather than the ultimacy or supremacy of God over the world, I follow the mystics' bewildering joy: In the beginning is intimacy and cocommunion. Here we sense the coalescing of the supernatural into the realm of the natural, impregnating all creation with the holy. The fusing or collapsing of identities that occurs in enlightenment or realization mystically repeats the event of the beginning where we are born out of that which is beyond name: the most intimate of intimacies. The spirituality that flows out of divine intimacy is directed toward preserving the communion of beings, so that no matter how far we stray, we always belong to God, to the beginning. We are held in a circle of belonging.

Global spirituality finds its center in the God of peace, in the spirituality of nonviolence, and in the Divine as intimate and benevolent. It is thus directed both in our inner lives and in the social environment toward healing of the historical oppression and marginalization inflicted by dominant theologies and philosophies on peoples, cultures, nations, and nature. Those with a vision of and commitment to the practice of global spirituality make a concerted effort to work toward the mending of inner divisions and outer enmities. All religious traditions advocate virtues of mercy and goodness. Like them, global spirituality is explicitly directed toward transforming the violence of the heart that exists in the individual and has been passed down through generations of religious seekers. Encoded in the religions of the world, in some form and in some way, is the root of religious violence. Disguised under conditions dictated by revelation or prophecy, and supported by histories, ancestors, traditions (both oral and written), theologies, and scriptures, religious violence infects our souls with a possessive and superior spirit. Justifying punishment, inquisitions, wars, moral superiority, and rigid or inflexible laws, religious violence is an illness in the human spirit that requires strong medicine and deep healing.

VI

My being is but a goblet in the Beloved's
hand—look at my eyes, if you do not believe it.[7]
   Rumi

    Like the founding movements of all new lineages, global spirituality is self-consciously constructive, borrowing resources from historical traditions and spiritual practices to articulate revelatory experiences. We might think of global spirituality as engaging the world in *"constructive mysticism."* I use this phrase to indicate that global consciousness utilizes traditional mystical thought and practice drawn from any religion or spiritual tradition to critically illuminate: (1) one's inner life, journey to divine realization or union, ways of knowing, and techniques of prayer and meditation; and (2) contemporary intellectual, psychological, social, political, and ethical concerns.

Global spirituality also uses contemporary critical methods drawn from the sciences and social sciences (feminism, postmodernism, quantum theory, ecology, liberation theology, and so forth) to illuminate traditional mystical or religious thought and practice. It does not merely adapt or adopt elements from our world religious heritage, but is critically attuned to oppressive elements in the social construction of religion, and actively works toward their alleviation in one's own spiritual life and in institutions, governments, and policies. It draws on new experiences of the sacred to reform elements in our collective consciousness that diminish or degrade the spiritual well-being of self and others. These oppressive elements are found wherever full dignity and equity of personhood is denied or suppressed.

In addition, this mystical engagement requires a choice: to conform and commit our lives to the freedom already granted to us in the beginning. It requires that we leave behind harmful or damaging aspects of our religious heritage and take the risk of embarking on a new spiritual road. This process is not easy, for to become truly awake to subtle dimensions of violence requires not only the intellect, psychology, and heart, but also the soul. Self-dignity involves a soul journey that suffers through and embodies the transformation of whatever is harmful, hurtful, or repressive in our religions and in our inner lives. We are taken through doubt and repentance and illumination and dark nights lived out not only in our own errors and sins, but also and explicitly in social and religious sins. In our interiority we feel how the intimacy of the Divine is violated or rejected in our world and how social and religious violence impact our spirits and the spirit of all of creation. We experience how human against human atrocities, our rapacious use of natural resources, and our wanton disregard for the integrity of the animal, plant, and mineral worlds damage our bodies and our souls. Global spirituality asserts that these planetary afflictions wound our hearts and distort our inner lives, leading to tragic consequences for our families, societies, the public good, and the earth as a whole.

If a spirituality centered on the unity of creation means anything, it must provide us with the resources to uncover and heal the hidden roots of religious violence. Only by paying careful attention to mending our own inner divisions, prejudices, and hates will we be able to help transform the world. In rare individuals like Gandhi, Day, Heschel, or Merton, we find evidence of critical engagement with the damaged roots of the religious imagination. Apostles of the God of peace, they conducted an ongoing and relentless inner critique of their personal imperfections and their religion's sins. They were in touch with a divine mission to the world: expand and embolden the human heart.

VII

> *You must love with the same pure love with*
> *which I love you.*[8]
> ↳—☙ Catherine of Siena

A new foundation for spirituality is available today. I think of it as mothering and feminine; and as a spirituality that is not tied to historical sins or religious punishments. It is the emergence of an expanded heart consciousness that is sensitizing us to the tragedy of our separateness, greed, violence, and pain. It is heart consciousness that rejoices in the mystical unity of life and suffers over the violation of the gentle, tender, and merciful. From the Eastern traditions, we have an understanding of the heart as the seat of nondual consciousness and fullness. It is a contemplative seeing of the One in everything; an awareness of life that allows us to perceive directly into the interdependence of all realities. In the Abrahamic mystical traditions, the heart is a spiritual organ that understands and perceives from a divine perspective. It is the core reality of the whole person made in the divine image and the seat of human compassion, empathy, and love. It is through the heart that the mystic in us comes into contact with a new life interpretation based on the unity of all creation. Even the word "unity" does not convey the vision that the heart sees, feels, and knows. It is too bland a word to evoke the wonder of belonging to all creation, from the invisible sub-atomic levels to the immeasurable expanse of space.

St. Gregory Palamas calls the heart "the shrine of the intelligence" and "the chief intellectual organ of the body." We think with our heart. Likewise, Ibn al' Arabi depicts the heart as a subtle organ of perception and the seat of knowledge of all the esoteric sciences. The power of the heart is a hidden force or energy that reflects the microcosmic form of the Divine. Thus, the mystical heart is the medium through which God not only is projected outward into the world, but it is also the eye by which God is revealed to God. As a spiritual organ, the heart is the seat of wisdom and the mediator between spirit and matter, divine and human. Integration takes place in the heart; in and through love all things are understood in a new way.

The divine spark in each thing is visible to the heart—the shining grandeur of Mystery here, now, shows us that all of creation is so many veils concealing God's presence. We are not abandoned or rejected. Separated by the thinnest of veils are little gossamer threads of spirit, binding us together in a tapestry of belonging everywhere present. The heart recognizes that this vision is not an approximation of what could be but the hidden unity within everything. The heart feels first and foremost the holy spark that animates everything. It cannot eliminate or suppress this sight.

An emerging heart means this: The future of life depends on expanding the capacity of the human heart. Our hearts are capable of loving more, giving more, and caring more for the world. Within us remains an untouched well of passion for life in which the Divine wounds us with love, expanding our capacity to love and feel exponentially. Illuminated in this way, our hearts are enflamed by the longing all around us to make the world a place where love may flourish. We need a heart philosophy and heart politics and religions that do not just talk about love but actualize spiritual love on earth. An emerging heart also implies that the Divine comes to us out of a hidden depth, an undisclosed dimension. It is a new creation, a new capacity within the human breast. But it is more than that. In the garden of our hearts, the Divine waters the seeds of a new revelation and a new wisdom nowhere abated. Joined with the weaving together of consciousness and cells, our adoration and our longing become an altar upon which the universe breathes its own prayer.

Global spirituality brings us back to the beginning, to be cocreators of a new earth consciousness. Back to the ancient stories within which our ancestors sinned and spoke. Back to the Garden of Eden and the biblical prohibition against knowledge and the punishment of females. Back to the sound of OM, the venerable mantric syllable. As a new divine-human venture, global spirituality refutes or pays no attention to the various and many attempts of religions to contain and control the

Mystery within their own specific and exclusive hierarchical structures. Instead, it goes back to the beginning to rectify the injustices and omissions of our collective religious heritage. It offers itself as a prayer of healing for the historical sins and institutional oppressions of our various religious worldviews. Only then—when we repent for our religious sins and support the dignity of all creation—will we have a "global" spirituality. Riding on the currents of free air, a global spiritual orientation follows this emerging heart to claim a new permission and a new realization of the intrinsic need to love and to be loved.

Acknowledgments

My deepest gratitude goes to Michael West, editor-in-chief of Fortress Press, for his vision, encouragement, and commitment to this project; and to Pamela Johnson, Bob Todd, and the rest of the publishing team at Fortress Press for their sincere dedication to theological inquiry. I am especially thankful that Michael asked Henry French to read and edit the final manuscript. Henry's care and wisdom made the process of completing *Emerging Heart* an inspiring experience.

Of course, this book would not have been written without the insights, questions, and brilliance of my many students, colleagues, and friends. To them, named and unnamed, I offer my appreciation for their sharing of the spiritual triumphs and trials that accompany every search for the holy. It is their stories of the heart's longing for God that inhabit and enliven the text.

My especial gratitude goes to my children, Maya, Gina, Tobin, and Shana Lanzetta, who sustain and uplift my heart on a daily basis; and to Shana for her detailed editing of an earlier version of the manuscript. It was her impassioned reading that furthered my decision to leave behind the academic voice and to write a personal narrative. My greatest thanks go to my husband, Bill Walton, whose love and support of my "inner monastery" make all of this possible.

Notes

1. Introduction

1. Pierre Teilhard de Chardin, *Hymn of the Universe* (New York: Harper and Row, 1965), 69.

2. Karl Jaspers, *The Origin and Goal of History*, trans. Michael Bullock (New Haven: Yale University Press, 1953), 2.

3. Ewert Cousins, *Process Thought on the Eve of the 21st Century*, The Alfred P. Stiernotte Lecture Series in Philosophy (Hamden, Conn.: Quinnipiac College, 1985), 14; idem., *Christ of the 21st Century* (Rockport, Mass.: Element, 1992), 7–10.

2. The Days of Awe

1. *Thomas Merton, Dialogues with Silence*, ed. Jonathan Montaldo (New York: HarperSanFrancisco, 2001), 5.

2. Rainer Maria Rilke, *Possibility of Being* (New York: New Directions, 1957, 1977), 70.

3. *Zohar: The Book of Enlightenment*, trans. Daniel Chanan Matt (New York: Paulist, 1983), 185.

4. For discussion of *"via feminina,"* see Beverly J. Lanzetta, *Radical Wisdom: A Feminist Mystical Theology* (Minneapolis: Fortress Press, 2005).

5. Dogen Zenji, cited in Robert Aiken, *The Mind of Clover: Essays in Zen Buddhist Ethics* (New York: North Point, 1984), 50.

6. *Hadjewijch: The Complete Works*, trans. Mother Columba Hart (New York: Paulist, 1980), 212.

7. Interfaith seminaries and interfaith chaplaincy are relatively new developments in religious history. Rabbi Joseph Gelberman established the first seminary of its kind in 1971 with the aid of clergy persons of many faith traditions. The school's mission was unique: to educate interfaith ministers and spiritual counselors to serve the needs of the world community. Rabbi Gelberman's motto, "Never instead, always in addition," summarizes the philosophy of interfaith training. In order to bring about spiritual reconciliation with our sisters and brothers of other religions, interfaith ministers are trained to honor the unity and diversity of traditions, rather than exclusion and difference.

8. *Bhagavad Gita* 11:37, trans. Juan Mascaro (New York: Penguin, 1962), 93.

3. Open Secrets

1. Cited in "Introduction," Norman Waddell, trans. *The Unborn: The Life and Teaching of Zen Master Bankei 1622–1693* (San Francisco: North Point, 1984), 5.

2. Ibid., 10.

3. Dorothy Day, cited in Jim Forest, "A Biography of Dorothy Day," http://www.catholicworker.com/ddaybio.htm.

4. Bernard McGinn, *The Foundations of Mysticism*. Volume 1 of *The Presence of God: A History of Western Christian Mysticism*. (New York: Crossroad, 1992), xix.

5. David Steindl-Rast, "The Great Circle Dance of the Religions," in *The Community of Religions: Voices and Images of the Parliament of the World's Religions* (New York: Continuum, 1996), 190.

6. Catherine of Siena, *The Dialogue*, trans. Suzanne Noffke (New York: Paulist, 1980), 169.

7. Tilopa, cited in *The Great Kagyu Masters: The Golden Lineage Treasury*, trans. Khenpo Konchog Gyaltsen (Ithaca, N.Y.: Snow Lion, 1990), 45.

4. One without Name

1. Edgar Mitchell, quoted in "Earth from Space," http://www.solarviews.com/eng/earthsp.htm.

2. Jelaluddin Rumi, "The Torrent Leaves," in *Open Secret: Versions of Rumi*, trans. John Moyne and Coleman Barks (Putney, Vt.: Threshold, 1984), 68.

3. Statistics are taken from the American Religious Identity Survey 2001. The full report is available at http://www.gc.cuny.edu/faculty/research_studies/aris.pdf.

4. Abraham Joshua Heschel, *The Sabbath: Its Meaning for Modern Man* (New York: Noonday, 1951, 1979), 74.

5. Rob Baker and Gray Henry, eds., *Merton and Sufism: The Untold Story* (Louisville: Fons Vitae, 1999), 65.

6. Ibid., 67.

7. Ibn al' Arabi, *Tarjuman al-Ashwaq*, in *The Mystics of Islam*, trans. Reynold A Nicholson http://wahiduddin.net/sufi/sufi_poetry.htm.

8. "Poem by Ramprasad," cited in Andrew Harvey, *The Return of the Mother* (New York: Jeremy P. Tarcher, 1995), 47.

5. In Search of Common Ground

1. Ewert H. Cousins, "My Journey into Interreligious Dialogue: Part I." Found online at Monastic Interreligious Dialogue, 2. http://monasticdialog.com/a.php?id=406&t=p.

2. Ibid., 3.

3. Mohandas K. Gandhi, *The Essential Gandhi: An Anthology of His Writings on His Life, Work, and Ideas*, ed. Louis Fischer, (New York: Vintage, 1983), 212.

4. Fernando Pessoa, cited online at http://www.geocities .com/idol911_4life/Pessoa.html.

5. Leonard Swidler, "Interreligious and Interideological Dialogue: The Matrix for all Systematic Reflection Today," in *Toward a Universal Theology of Religion*, ed. Leonard Swidler (Maryknoll, N.Y.: Orbis, 1987), 6.

6. Ibid., 17.

7. John Dunne, *The Way of All the Earth* (Notre Dame, Ind.: University of Notre Dame Press, 1978), ix.

8. Ewert Cousins labels the ability to enter into spiritual realities of other peoples and traditions a "shamanistic epistemology." See Ewert H. Cousins, "Interreligious Dialogue: The Spiritual Journey of Our Time," *IRF: A Newsletter of the International Religious Foundation, Inc.* Vol. 2: idem, *Christ of the 21st Century* (Rockport, Mass.: Element, 1992), especially 105–31.

9. For further development of his ground-breaking insights into cocreative participation, see Jorge Ferrer, *Revisioning Transpersonal Psychology: A Participatory Vision of Human Spirituality* (Albany: SUNY Press, 2002), 118–21.

10. Raimon Panikkar, "Faith and Belief: A Multireligious Experience," *Anglican Theological Review* 53 (1971): 220.

11. Raimon Panikkar's many contributions to interreligious dialogue include *Blessed Simplicity: The Monk as Universal Archetype* (New York: Seabury, 1982); *The Unknown Christ of Hinduism* (Maryknoll, N.Y.: Orbis, 1981); *The Silence of God: The Answer of the Buddha* (Maryknoll, N.Y.: Orbis, 1989); *The Trinity and the Religious Experience of Man* (Maryknoll, N.Y.: Orbis, 1973); *The Cosmotheandric Experience: Emerging Religious Consciousness.* Maryknoll, N.Y.: Orbis, 1993; and *The Intra-Religious Dialogue* (New York: Paulist, 1999).

12. Abraham Joshua Heschel, "No Religion Is an Island," cited in Harold Kasimow, ed., *No Religion Is an Island: Abraham Joshua Heschel and Interreligious Dialogue* (Maryknoll, N.Y.: Orbis, 1991), 14.

13. Ewert H. Cousins, "My Journey into Interreligious Dialogue," 3.

14. Ewert H. Cousins, "For it may well be that the meeting of spiritual paths—the assimilation not only of one's own spiritual heritage but of that of the human community as a whole—is the distinctive spiritual journey of our time." "Preface" to the multivolume series *World Spirituality: An Encyclopedic History of the Religious Quest* (New York: Company, 1987–), xiv

6. Communion That Surpasses Words

1. Thomas Merton, *The Monastic Journey*, Patrick Hart, ed. (New York: Image, 1978), 61.

2. See Wayne Teasdale, *The Mystic Heart: Discovering a Universal Spirituality in the World's Religions* (Novato, Calif.: New World Library, 1999).

3. Paul Elie, *The Life You Save May Be Your Own: An American Pilgrimage* (New York: Farrar, Straus, Giroux, 2003), 416.

4. Miguel de Unamuno, *The Tragic Sense of Life in Men and Nations*, trans. Anthony Kerrigan (Princeton: Princeton University Press, 1972), 150.

5. Robert Inchausti, *Thomas Merton's American Prophecy* (Albany: SUNY Press, 1998), 71.

6. Thomas Merton, "Preface to the Japanese Edition of *Seeds of Contemplation*," in Robert E. Daggy, ed., *Thomas Merton: Introductions East and West* (Greensboro, N.C.: Unicorn, 1981), 66.

7. Inchausti, *Thomas Merton's American Prophecy*, 150–51.

8. *Majihima-nikaya*, 1:161. Cited in Raimon Panikkar, *The Silence of God: The Answer of the Buddha* (Maryknoll, NY: Orbis, 1989), 167.

9. Thomas Merton, *Disputed Questions* (New York: Harcourt, Brace, Jovanovich, 1960), 207.

10. Thomas Merton, *The Asian Journal of Thomas Merton*, ed. Naomi Burton, Patrick Hart, and James Laughlin (New York: New Directions, 1973, 1977), 314.

11. Ibid., 315–16.

12. Dogen, *Zen Master Dogen: An Introduction with Selected Writings*, Yuho Yokoi, ed. (New York: Weatherhill,) 69–70.

13. Monastic Interreligious Dialogue, http://monasticdialog.com/mid.php?id=10.

14. Excerpt of prayer, written by His Holiness the Dalai Lama, http://www.tibet.com/DL/truth.html.

15. Leonard Swidler, "Pluralism and Oppression: Dialogue between the Many Religions and the Many Poor," *The*

Community of Religions, eds. Wayne Teasdale and George Cairns (New York: Continuum, 1996), 200.

16. Ibid., 201.

17. Mohandas K. Gandhi, *Prayer,* ed. John Strohmeier (Berkeley, Calif.: Berkeley Hills, 2000), 41.

18. Martin Luther King Jr., *A Testament of Hope: The Essential Writings and Speeches of Martin Luther King, Jr.,* ed. James M. Washington (San Francisco: HarperSanFrancisco, 1986), 447.

19. Leo Tolstoy, http://www.soulforce.org/article/636.

20. See Mohandas K. Gandhi, *Vows and Observances,* ed. John Strohmeier (Berkeley, Calif.: Berkeley Hills, 1999), especially "The Eleven Observances," and "The Ashram Vows," 29–48.

21. Martin Luther King Jr., http://www.soulforce.org/article/636.

22. Pseudo-Dionysius, *Pseudo-Dionysius: The Complete Works,* trans. Colm Luibheid (New York: Paulist, 1987), 121.

23. Merton, *Asian Journal,* 308.

7. Emerging Heart

1. Thomas Merton, *A Thomas Merton Reader,* ed. Thomas P. McDonnell (New York: Image, 1974), 512.

2. Mahadeviyakka, cited in *Women in Praise of the Sacred: 43 Centuries of Spiritual Poetry by Women,* ed. Jane Hirshfield (New York: HarperCollins, 1994), 81.

3. *Meister Eckhart: Sermons and Treatises,* trans. and ed. M. O'C. Walshe, vol. 1, sermon 9 (Longmead, Eng.: Element, 1979), 83–85

4. *Sefer ha-Bahir,* cited in Gershom Scholem, *On the Mystical Shape of the Godhead* (New York: Schocken, 1991), 98.

5. Gregory of Nyssa, *From Glory to Glory: Texts from Gregory of Nyssa's Mystical Writings*, trans. Herbert Musurillo (Crestwood, N.Y.: St. Vladimir's Seminary Press, 1979), 32–33.

6. Julian of Norwich, *Julian of Norwich: Showings* (New York: Paulist, 1978), 191.

7. Jalal ah-din Rumi, *Mystical Poems of Rumi*, trans. A. J. Arberry (Chicago: University of Chicago Press, 1968), 50.

8. Catherine of Siena, *The Dialogue*, trans. Suzanne Noffke (New York: Paulist, 1980), 165.

Bibliography

Aitken, Robert, and David Steindl-Rast. *The Ground We Share: Everyday Practice, Buddhist and Christian.* New York: Shambhala, 1996.

Armstrong, Karen. *The Great Transformation: The Beginning of Our Religious Traditions.* New York: Alfred Knopf, 2006.

Barnhart, Bruno, and Joseph Wong, eds. *Purity of Heart and Contemplation: A Monastic Dialogue between Christian and Buddhist Traditions.* New York: Continuum, 1991.

Bruteau, Beatrice. *The Other Half of My Soul: Bede Griffiths and the Hindu-Christian Dialogue.* Wheaton, Ill.: Quest Books, 1996.

Cairns, George, and Wayne Teasdale. *The Community of Religions: Voices and Images of the Parliament of the World's Religions.* New York: Continuum, 1996.

Chase, Steven L. *Doors of Understanding: Conversations on Global Spirituality in Honor of Ewert Cousins.* Quincy, Ill.: Franciscan Press, 1997.

Chittister, Joan. *In Search of Belief.* Liguori, Mo.: Liguori Publications, 1999.

_____. *Seeing with Our Souls: Monastic Wisdom for Everyday.* New York: Sheed and Ward, 2002.

_____. *There Is a Season.* Maryknoll, N.Y.: Orbis Books, 1995.

Cobb, John B., Jr., and Christopher Ives, eds. *The Emptying God: A Buddhist-Jewish-Christian Conversation.* Maryknoll, N.Y.: Orbis Books, 1990.

Colledge, Edmund, and Bernard McGinn, trans. and eds. *Meister Eckhart The Essential Sermons, Commentaries, and Defense.* New York: Paulist Press, 1981.

Corless, Roger, and Paul F. Knitter, eds. *Buddhist Emptiness and Christian Trinity: Essays and Explorations.* New York: Paulist Press, 1990.

Cousins, Ewert H. *Christ of the 21st Century.* Continuum, 1994.

_____. *Global Spirituality: Toward the Meeting of Mystical Paths.* Madras, India: Radhakrishnan Institute for Advanced Study in Philosophy, University of Madras, 1985.

Culligan, Kevin, et al. *Purifying the Heart: Buddhist Insight Meditation for Christians.* New York: Crossroad, 1994.

Dalai Lama. *Ethics for the New Millennium.* New York: Riverhead Books, 1999.

_____. *The Good Heart: A Buddhist Perspective on the Teachings of Jesus.* Boston, Mass.: Wisdom Publications, 1996.

Davie, Ian. *Jesus Purusha: A Vedanta-Based Doctrine of Jesus.* West Stockbridge, Mass.: Inner Traditions/Lindisfarne Press, 1985.

Dryer, Elizabeth, and Mark Burrows, eds. *Minding the Spirit: The Study of Christian Spirituality.* Johns Hopkins University Press, 2005.

Eck, Diana L. *Encountering God: A Spiritual Journey from Bozeman to Banaras.* Boston: Beacon Press, 1992.

Fox, Matthew, trans. *Breakthrough: Meister Eckhart's Creation Spirituality in New Translation.* New York: Doubleday, 1980.

_____. *Original Blessing: A Primer in Creation Spirituality.* Santa Fe: Bear, 1983.

Griffiths, Bede. *Return to the Center.* Springfield, Ill.: Templegate, 1987.

_____. *River of Compassion: A Christian Reading of the Bhagavad Gita.* New York: Continuum, 1987.

Hanh, Thich Nhat. *Being Peace.* Berkeley, Calif.: Parallax Press, 1987.

_____. *Living Buddha, Living Christ.* New York: Riverhead Books, 1995.

Hart, Patrick et al., eds. *The Asian Journal of Thomas Merton.* New York: New Directions, 1973.

Henry, Patrick, ed. *Benedict's Dharma: Buddhists Reflect on the Rule of Saint Benedict.* New York: Riverhead Books, 2001.

Heschel, Abraham Joshua. *God in Search of Man.* New York: Farrar, Straus, and Giroux, 1955.

_____. *The Prophets.* 2 vols. New York: Harper and Row, 1962.

Heschel, Susannah, ed. *Moral Grandeur and Spiritual Audacity: Abraham Joshua Heschel.* New York: Farrar, Straus, and Giroux, 1996.

Hick, John. *God Has Many Names.* Philadelphia: Westminster Press, 1980, 1982.

_____. *An Interpretation of Religion: Human Responses to the Transcendent.* New Haven: Yale University Press, 1989.

Hick, John and Paul F. Knitter, eds. *The Myth of Christian Uniqueness: Toward a Pluralistic Theology of Religions.* Maryknoll, N.Y.: Orbis Books, 1987.

Idel, Moshe and Bernard McGinn. *Mystical Union and Monotheistic Faith: An Ecumenical Dialogue.* New York: Macmillan, 1989.

James, William. *The Varieties of Religious Experience: A Study in Human Nature.* New York: Modern Library, 1999.

Johnston, William. *Mystical Theology: The Science of Love.* Maryknoll, N.Y.: Orbis Books, 1995.

_____. *The Still Point, Reflections on Zen and Christian Mysticism.* New York: Fordham University Press, 1982.

Kamenetz, Rodger. *The Jew in the Lotus: A Poet's Rediscovery of Jewish Identity in Buddhist India.* San Francisco: Harper Collins, 1994.

_____. *Stalking Elijah: Adventures with Today's Jewish Mystical Masters.* San Francisco: HarperSanFrancisco, 1997.

Kasimow, Harold, and Byron Sherwin. *No Religion Is an Island: Abraham Joshua Heschel and Interreligious Dialogue.* Maryknoll, N.Y.: Orbis Books, 1991.

Keenan, John P. *The Meaning of Christ: A Mahayana Theology.* Maryknoll, N.Y.: Orbis Books, 1989.

King, Ursula. *Women and Spirituality: Voices of Protest and Promise.* University Park: Pennsylvania University Press, 1989, 1993.

Knitter, Paul. *No Other Name? A Critical Survey of Christian Attitudes toward the World Religions.* Maryknoll, N.Y.: Orbis Books, 1985.

Küng, Hans. *Christianity and the World Religions: Paths of Dialogue with Islam, Hinduism, and Buddhism.* Garden City, N.Y.: Doubleday, 1986.

_____. *Theology for the Third Millenium: An Ecumenical View.* Trans. Peter Heinegg. New York: Doubleday, 1988.

Lanzetta, Beverly. *The Other Side of Nothingness: Toward a Theology of Radical Openness.* Albany, N.Y.: State University of New York Press, 2001.

_____. *Path of the Heart.* New York: Paragon House, 1996.

_____. *Radical Wisdom: A Feminist Mystical Theology.* Minneapolis: Fortress Press, 2005.

Lew, Alan, with Sherril Jaffe. *One God Clapping: The Spiritual Path of a Zen Rabbi.* New York: Kodansha International, 1999.

McGinn, Bernard, ed. and trans. *Meister Eckhart: Teacher and Preacher.* The Classics of Western Spirituality. New York: Paulist Press, 1986.

Merton, Thomas. *Contemplation in a World of Action.* New York: Doubleday, 1973.

_____. *Mystics and Zen Masters.* New York: Farrar, Straus and Giroux, 1967.

_____. *The Way of Chuang Tzu.* New York: New Directions, 1969.

_____. *Zen and the Birds of Appetite.* New York: New Directions, 1969.

Mitchell, Donald W. *Spirituality and Emptiness: The Dynamics of Spiritual Life in Buddhism and Christianity.* Mahwah, N.J.: Paulist Press, 1991.

_____ and James Wiseman, eds. *The Gethsemani Encounter: A Dialogue on the Spiritual Life by Buddhist and Christian Monastics.* New York: Continuum, 1999.

_____ and James Wiseman, eds. *Transforming Suffering: Reflections on Finding Peace in Troubled Times by His Holiness the Dalai Lamma, His Holiness Pope John Paul II, Thomas Keating, Joseph Goldstein, Thubten Chodro.* New York: Image Books, 2003.

Nasr, Seyyed Hossein. *Sufi Essays.* New York: Schocken Books, 1977.

Otto, Rudolf. *The Idea of the Holy.* New York: Oxford University Press, 1958.

Panikkar, Raimon. *Blessed Simplicity: The Monk as Universal Archetype.* New York: Seabury Press, 1982.

_____. *The Cosmotheandric Experience: Emerging Religious Consciousness.* Maryknoll, N.Y.: Orbis Books, 1993.

_____. *The Intra-Religious Dialogue.* New York: Paulist Press, 1978.

_____. *The Silence of God: The Answer of the Buddha.* Maryknoll, N.Y.: Orbis Books, 1989.

Swidler, Leonard, ed. *Toward a Universal Theology of Religion.* Maryknoll, N.Y.: Orbis Books, 1987.

Teasdale, Wayne R. *A Monk in the World: Cultivating a Spiritual Life.* Novato, Calif.: New World Library, 2002.

_____. *The Mystic Heart: Discovering a Universal Spirituality in the World's Religions.* Novato, Calif.: New World Library, 1999.

_____ and George Cairns, eds. *The Community of Religions: Voices and Images of the Parliament of the World's Religions.* New York: Continuum, 1996.

Teilhard de Chardin, Pierre. *Hymn of the Universe*. New York: Harper and Row, 1965.

Underhill, Evelyn. *Mysticism: A Study in the Nature and Development of Spiritual Consciousness*. Dover Publications, 2002.

Walshe, M. O'C., trans. and ed. *Meister Eckhart: Sermons and Treatises*. Volumes I–III. Longmead, Eng.: Element Books, 1979.

Also of interest from Fortress Press

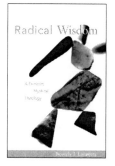
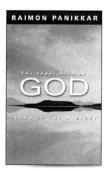